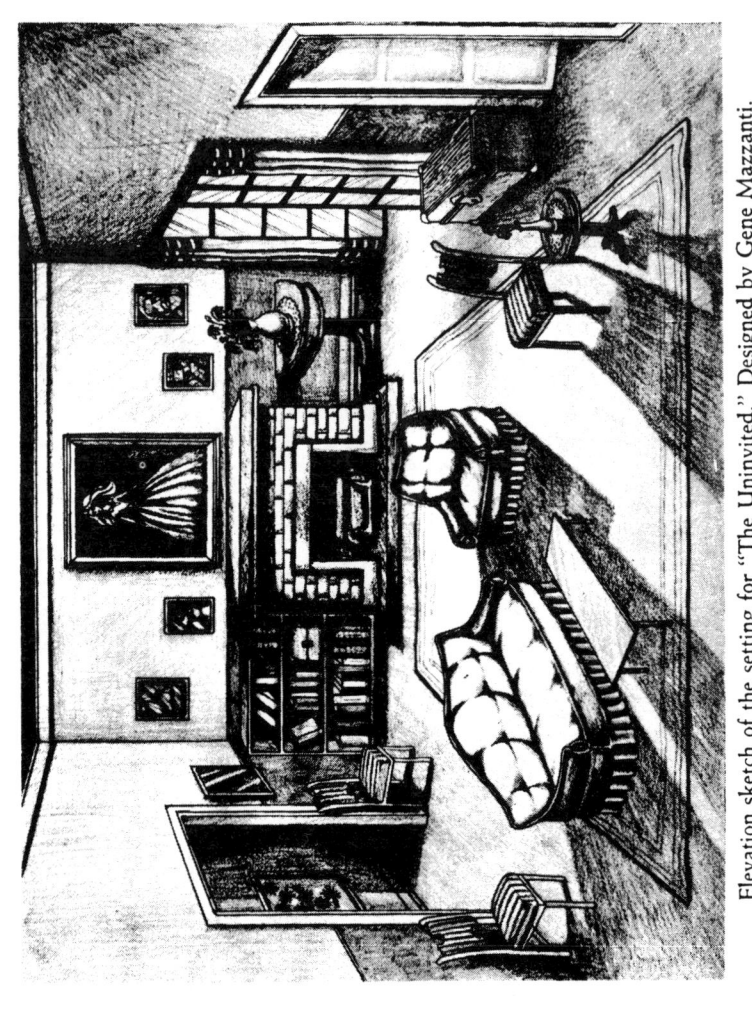

Elevation sketch of the setting for "The Uninvited." Designed by Gene Mazzanti.

THE UNINVITED

DOROTHY MACARDLE'S
CLASSIC GHOST STORY

A PLAY IN THREE ACTS
BY TIM KELLY

★

★

DRAMATISTS
PLAY SERVICE
INC.

THE UNINVITED
Copyright © 1979, Tim Kelly and Donald Macardle

based on Dorothy Macardle's novel *The Uninvited*
Copyright © 1942, Dorothy Macardle

All Rights Reserved

SPECIAL NOTE

STORY OF THE PLAY

Pam Fitzgerald and her brother Roddy, an aspiring playwright, discover an abandoned but charming house in the west of England overlooking the Irish Sea. The house is Cliff End and they are able to purchase it at a suspiciously low price from crusty Commander Brooke, the village curmudgeon. The reason is quickly apparent. The house has an unsavory reputation. Fifteen years earlier a murder may or may not have occurred by the gnarled tree that can be viewed from the parlor window. Slowly, the Fitzgeralds begin to sense the evil spirit that announces its presence by permeating the house with a bone-chilling cold. The housekeeper's cat will not enter the nursery where the sound of a weeping woman adds to the tense atmosphere and the scent of a flowery, exotic perfume called *mimosa* comes and goes. The village doctor, the local gossip, and a former governess visit with strange stories of the beautiful Mary Meredith who once lived in the house and the unstable Carmel who posed for a painting that destroyed her. With the help of Mary's daughter, Stella, a beautiful young girl whose mysterious birth is the puzzle's key, and a seance arranged by an actress friend of the Fitzgeralds, who has mediumistic gifts, Cliff End is forced to reveal its darkest secrets. The action eventually builds to a truly terrifying climax when the ghost is discovered to be not only real, but *dangerous*. The production requirements are simple, and the special effects, easily handled, will fascinate the audience. Each of the ten roles offers an excellent opportunity for characterization. This is a genuine romantic stage thriller that takes its ghost seriously. Adapted from the acclaimed novel by Dorothy Macardle, *The Uninvited* was made into a highly-successful Paramount film starring Ray Milland, Cornelia Otis Skinner, Ruth Hussey and Gail Russell.

A play in Three Acts
For Six Women and Four Men

CHARACTERS
(In Order of Appearance)

STELLA MEREDITH, about 18, charming but vulnerable

PAMELA FITZGERALD, mid-20's, intelligent and enthusiastic

RODDY FITZGERALD, Pamela's brother, older by a year or two, an aspiring playwright

COMMANDER BROOKE, Stella's grandfather, stern and overprotective

LIZZIE FLYNN, Pam and Roddy's housekeeper, loyal but superstitious

MRS. JESSUP, a neighbor and gossip

WENDY, a vivacious young actress

MAX HILLIARD, a young painter, friend of the Fitzgeralds

DR. SCOTT, pleasant, middle-aged, village doctor

MISS HOLLOWAY, Stella's former nurse and governess, cold and slightly sinister

and

THE UNINVITED

SYNOPSIS

The action of the play takes place in the sitting room of Cliff End, an isolated house overlooking the Bristol Channel in the west of England. The time is the present.

ACT I

Scene 1: A late summer morning.

Scene 2: Some weeks later. Afternoon.

ACT II

Scene 1: Two weeks later. Evening.

Scene 2: The following morning.

ACT III

That evening.

THE UNINVITED

ACT I

SCENE 1

SETTING: *A comfortable sitting room or parlor in Cliff End, a house overlooking the Bristol Channel in the west of England.*
Right is an empty hallway that leads in from other, unseen, quarters of the house. There is a chair on each side of the entry. Up Center there is a substantial fireplace and on the wall above a painting of an extremely beautiful woman, a former occupant of the house. This is Mary Meredith, a composed and elegant creature with blue eyes, all in white, with long, fair hair.
Left are French doors that open onto a small patio and the offstage expanse of lawn that stretches to the edge of the cliff. There are drapes or curtains that can be drawn across when necessary. Down Left is a door that leads into a room that was once used as a nursery.
Down Right we find a small sofa and a low table in front of it. To the Left of the sofa is a comfortable armchair. Down Left Center is another chair with a small table to one side.
To these basic properties should be added logical stage dressing. Pictures, lamps or wall sconces, rugs, other chairs, etc.
The time is the present.

AT RISE: *The house has stood vacant for some time. White sheets cover the sofa and chairs.*
Stella Meredith, about eighteen, is drawing aside the curtains. She opens the French doors and as she does, a bright burst of sunshine floods into the room, banishing shadows. Sound of sea birds can be heard in the distance.

7

STELLA. There. That's better. Sunlight always helps. (*Stella is a lovely girl, rather childlike, but her manner, at times, would be appropriate in a hostess of thirty. She is clearly excited about something.*) Oh, the sheets! (*Quickly, she moves to the sofa and begins to remove the white covering.*) PAM. (*Offstage.*) Miss Meredith? Where are you? Miss Meredith? STELLA. In here, Miss Fitzgerald. PAM. (*Offstage.*) Where? STELLA. The sitting room. (*She rolls up the sheet. In a moment, Pamela Fitzgerald enters R. She's in her twenties, bright, intelligent, inclined to be both impulsive and enthusiastic.*) PAM. The house is charming. Quite charming. STELLA. You do like it, then? PAM. I adore it. STELLA. I hoped you would. (*As they converse, Stella removes more of the sheets in an attempt to show the room to its best advantage.*) PAM. It's a lonely spot. Of course, a writer has to be able to be alone, and I make friends easily. STELLA. There's a wonderful view from the patio, but I'm afraid the garden has gone to weed. PAM. That is a pity. STELLA. Gardens do need love and care. (*Pam crosses to the French doors, stares out.*) PAM. I'm quite good in a garden. I don't have much opportunity in London. STELLA. I didn't know you were a writer, Miss Fitzgerald. PAM. I'm not. My brother has most of the creative talent. He's quite a good literary critic, but he's decided to go out on a limb. STELLA. How do you mean? PAM. He's writing a play. STELLA. (*Impressed*) I imagine that's terribly exciting. PAM. Not to hear Roddy tell it. He equates it with a kind of mental torture. (*Savors the view.*) The lawn sweeps straight to the edge of the cliff. Breathtaking. I imagine the winds can be devilish. STELLA. The house is fairly well protected. It's sheltered by a wooded rise on the east and on the north there's a windbreak of trees. PAM. I suppose your grandfather would want an arm and a leg. STELLA. I never discuss things like that with Grandfather. He

8

doesn't have much faith in me, I'm afraid. (*By now Stella has removed most of the white coverings and placed them in a neat pile on a chair near the entry.*)

PAM. You impress me as a most capable young woman.

STELLA. (*Pleased.*) I am, I imagine. In some things.

PAM. Do you like living in the village?

STELLA. It's a bit strange to me. I've been away, you see. To school. In Brussels. (*Pam sees the portrait above the fireplace mantle, crosses to it.*)

PAM. The village is too quiet for you?

STELLA. Oh, no. I like Biddlecombe. (*Looks about the room.*) I like being close to this house. I'm always happy when I can look up from the village and see Cliff End. (*Wistful.*) Sometimes I get the feeling the house beckons to me.

PAM. You have quite an imagination, Miss Meredith. You'll have to have a long talk with my brother.

STELLA. Won't you call me Stella? Miss Meredith sounds so formal. I do hope we're going to be friends.

PAM. (*Indicates painting.*) Who is she?

STELLA. (*Smiles warmly, moves to fireplace.*) My mother.

PAM. (*Surprised.*) Then this was your mother's home?

STELLA. Yes. My father painted that portrait. You may have heard of him. He was fairly well known. Llewellyn Meredith.

PAM. (*Thinks.*) I don't recognize the name. (*Studies portrait.*) He loved your mother deeply. It shows in his work.

STELLA. Oh, yes. They were very much in love.

PAM. You'll have to excuse me if I ask too many questions, Stella. Roddy says I'm nosey. He's right. I've never been able to conquer curiosity.

STELLA. What did you want to ask?

PAM. I take it your mother's dead?

STELLA. Yes.

PAM. Your father, too?

STELLA. Yes. Mother died in an . . . "accident," and Father drowned when his boat overturned during a storm. That was fifteen years ago. Grandfather's brought me up.

RODDY. (*Offstage.*) Pam!

PAM. I'm here, Roddy. (*Roderick Fitzgerald enters* R. *He's practical, intelligent, a year or two older than his sister.*)

9

RODDY. There are two or three small storerooms behind the kitchen. That would please Lizzie.
STELLA. Lizzie?
PAM. She practically raised us. Lizzie Flynn is a combination nanny, cook, nurse—
RODDY. —and fulltime gossip.
PAM. You wouldn't say that if she were here with us now. (*To Stella.*) Apart from everything else, Lizzie has an Irish temper. (*Stella moves behind sofa.*)
STELLA. Your Lizzie Flynn will be happy here. I know she will.
RODDY. We're not certain we're taking the house.
STELLA. Oh. but you must. (*To Pam.*) You did say you liked it.
PAM. I do, Stella, but there are other considerations.
STELLA. If you took the house I could come and visit you, couldn't I?
PAM. Certainly.
STELLA. I wouldn't be much trouble and I wouldn't come unless invited.
RODDY. That isn't the point. I wonder if I might have a few words with my sister alone. Would you mind, Miss Meredith?
STELLA. I'll be upstairs in my mother's room. (*Crosses R., turns.*) You mustn't call me Miss Meredith. You must call me Stella—as your sister does. (*With feeling.*) We'll be the best of friends. (*Stella exits.*)
RODDY. Pretty thing, isn't she?
PAM. I thought you'd notice. She wants us to have the house. She's almost desperate on that point.
RODDY. You two seem to have gotten on. What did she mean— "mother's room"?
PAM. Seems Cliff End was her parents' home. (*Indicates portrait.*) That's Stella's mother. Beautiful, wasn't she? (*He looks.*)
RODDY. I wonder why Stella didn't mention it before we got here?
PAM. You saw the excited state she was in. She could barely get the key in the front door, her hand was shaking so. (*Pam sits D. L. C.*) Roderick, it *is* a lovely house.
RODDY. Don't call me Roderick. Whenever you call me Roderick, you plan to persuade me about something or other. (*He moves D. C.*)
PAM. It's the sort of place we've been looking for.
RODDY. You haven't looked at this place as closely as I have.

10

The plumbing's not all it might be, the wiring looks faulty. This seems to be the only spot that's livable. The ceiling in the living room is peeling, one wall is cracked, and the dining room is eaten with dry rot.

PAM. Dry rot? You call yourself a writer? Where's your vision? One must consider the possibilities beyond dry rot. (*Leans forward.*) I bet we could lease it for a song.

RODDY. Lease! Absolutely not. We'd have to paint and carpenter, plant and dig every spare minute for somebody else.

PAM. Can we afford to buy?

RODDY. (*Ponders.*) Lot of work to be done and the house has been idle for who knows how long.

PAM. That should work in our favor.

RODDY. There's a bare chance that it might be within our price.

PAM. Think of it. To own soil and rocks and trees and a beach.

RODDY. Don't get carried away. If this place hasn't sold there must be a reason.

PAM. The isolation.

RODDY. Or the price.

PAM. You might try being more optimistic. We both agreed we wanted to get out of London.

RODDY. I didn't mean two hundred miles out.

PAM. Bristol's close. It has a decent theatre season. You won't have to give up anything you cherish. Besides, you could always take the train or the car into London.

RODDY. You *do* have your heart set on this place.

PAM. I had almost made up my mind that what we wanted didn't exist.

RODDY. I have my work. I don't want to spend all my time hammering and restoring.

PAM. You won't have to. Leave all that to me. We'll go one room at a time. I'd love to decorate this place. Please talk to Stella's grandfather.

RODDY. (*Gives up.*) I'll call him this evening.

COMMANDER BROOKE. That won't be necessary, Mr. Fitz-gerald. (*Commander Brooke has entered from the garden. He's elderly, carries a walking stick, has the air of a man going into battle.*)

RODDY. You're Commander Brooke?

11

COMMANDER BROOKE. I am. I would have appreciated it if you had waited for me.

PAM. (*Stands.*) We would have waited, but your granddaughter was anxious to accommodate us.

COMMANDER BROOKE. Stella had no business coming here. She's a highly emotional girl and Cliff End only upsets her.

RODDY. If we had known that we never would have permitted her to show us the house.

COMMANDER BROOKE. Too late now. My housekeeper tells me you're from London.

RODDY. Yes. I'm a writer. Criticism, mostly.

PAM. You may have seen my brother's name in print. He's prolific.

COMMANDER BROOKE. I'm afraid I don't read criticism. (*Pam and Roddy look at one another in mild despair. Stella's grandfather will be a tough nut to crack.*)

PAM. (*Smiles in an attempt to be friendly.*) May I offer you a chair in your own home, Commander Brooke? (*She gestures to the* D. L. C. *chair.*)

COMMANDER BROOKE. Thank you. I walked up from the village. I'm not in the best of health, so I thought the exercise might prove beneficial. I may have overdone it. (*He crosses, sits. Pam moves to sofa, sits.*)

PAM. You have a charming place here.

RODDY. (*Anxious to keep the price down.*) But run down. The upstairs especially.

PAM. (*Catching on.*) And the plumbing— (*Looks to Roddy remembering his words.*) it's not all it might be.

COMMANDER BROOKE. Except for a brief period of a few months, the house has been untenanted for sometime.

RODDY. How long?

COMMANDER BROOKE. Fifteen years. The roof badly needs repairs. However, it's a well-built house. The man who designed it was an architect and had it built for himself. Five generations of my family lived here in health and comfort. Considerable sums were spent on improvements about twenty-four years ago.

RODDY. Time takes a toll on buildings.

COMMANDER BROOKE. The house is for sale, Mr. Fitzgerald. (*Hard.*) As is.

PAM. (*Eager to soften the mood.*) Commander? That implies the navy.

12

COMMANDER BROOKE. Retired.

RODDY. My sister and I are not wealthy and the house is going to require work.

COMMANDER BROOKE. I will consider an offer, but I must point out that the house belongs to my granddaughter. However, she will abide by my wishes in this matter. (*Roddy takes out a small notebook and pencil, writes down some figure. He rips off the sheet, shows it to Pam, passes it to Commander Brooke. He takes it and studies the offering price, no expression gives a hint of his reaction, until:*) This is your final offer?

RODDY. With the house in its present condition, I'm afraid it is. (*The silence is almost electric as Commander Brooke continues to stare at the sheet of paper.*)

COMMANDER BROOKE. This will do.

PAM. (*Not certain she understands.*) You'll sell?

COMMANDER BROOKE. Yes.

RODDY. (*Points to paper.*) At that price?

COMMANDER BROOKE. There's a good man at my bank in Barnstaple. He can handle all the arrangements if you'd like. (*Roddy and Pam can't believe their good luck. They're in a state of minor shock.*)

PAM. Whatever you suggest. By all means.

COMMANDER BROOKE. Would you get my granddaughter, Miss Fitzgerald? She must be somewhere about.

PAM. I'll find her. (*Pam exits R.*)

RODDY. I understand this was your daughter's home.

COMMANDER BROOKE. (*Looks to painting.*) Mary. Yes.

RODDY. You'll want the portrait, of course.

COMMANDER BROOKE. That was painted by my daughter's husband. I prefer the one I have in my own cottage.

RODDY. Stella will want it, then.

COMMANDER BROOKE. The house is for sale with all its contents, Mr. Fitzgerald, including that portrait. If you don't wish it on the wall, I suggest you store it somewhere. There's considerable space in the attic. (*Roddy realizes he's getting into deep water, is eager to shift the conversation, sees door D. L.*)

RODDY. Hello. What's that? Another room? (*He crosses to it.*)

COMMANDER BROOKE. I will ask that you not encourage Stella to visit Cliff End. Her constitution is not strong. There are only sad memories for my granddaughter here.

RODDY. She's anxious to make friends.

COMMANDER BROOKE. Stella can be a most charming girl when she chooses. (*Roddy tries the door. It doesn't give. He tries again.*)

RODDY. It's locked. I suppose Stella has the key.

COMMANDER BROOKE. No.

RODDY. I hope we won't have to force the lock.

COMMANDER BROOKE. That won't be necessary. I'll see that you receive the key. (*Stella and Pam enter* R. *Stella nervously twists a handkerchief. Her grandfather's arrival is unsettling.*)

STELLA. You know the doctor has warned you against exertion, Grandfather.

COMMANDER BROOKE. (*Stands.*) If you had not disobeyed my wishes and come here, perhaps the exertion could have been avoided. (*To Roddy.*) I don't drive.

STELLA. (*Moves* D. C.) I was afraid we might lose a prospective buyer.

COMMANDER BROOKE. (*Hint of anger.*) Don't be devious, Stella.

STELLA. (*Contrite.*) I didn't mean to be. (*He sniffs.*)

COMMANDER BROOKE. You have mimosa on that handkerchief. (*Quickly Stella pockets it.*)

STELLA. I am sorry, Grandfather. I forgot how much you dislike my perfume.

COMMANDER BROOKE. I supposed that you had forgotten. (*Pam moves behind sofa, tries for a note of pleasantness.*)

PAM. Could we all have dinner together this evening? We're staying at the inn. You'll be our guests, of course. Since we're buying the house, it'll be something of a celebration.

RODDY. Splendid idea.

COMMANDER BROOKE. No, you must be our guests. How's the larder, Stella? Can we give ourselves the pleasure of inviting our new acquaintances to dinner?

STELLA. (*Delighted.*) Yes, yes!

COMMANDER BROOKE. Go along, Stella. I'll meet you at the gate.

PAM. You must let us drive you back to the village.

COMMANDER BROOKE. The walk will do Stella good. I imagine you will want to explore more of the house on your own. (*Insists.*)

14

Go along, Stella. I'll only be a moment. (*Stella moves to the French doors.*)

STELLA. I hope you'll be happy in the house.

RODDY. I'm sure we will.

STELLA. I *know* you will. (*She exits. Roddy moves to* D. L. C. *chair.*)

PAM. The air at Cliff End must be superb.

COMMANDER BROOKE. There is the occasional wind storm.

RODDY. My sister and I are partial to storms.

COMMANDER BROOKE. The wind makes melancholy sounds, blowing over the moors.

PAM. That won't worry us. (*Commander Brooke seems to be driving at something. He speaks abruptly.*)

COMMANDER BROOKE. A clear duty is imposed on me.

RODDY. Yes?

COMMANDER BROOKE. I told you the house was occupied for some months.

PAM. When was that?

COMMANDER BROOKE. Six years ago. I must inform you that the people did not stay very long.

RODDY. Why was that? (*Commander Brooke pauses before he speaks.*)

COMMANDER BROOKE. They "experienced" disturbances here. (*Roddy and Pam are intrigued.*)

RODDY. Ah. the house has a legend.

COMMANDER BROOKE. I have no idea what you're referring to. Mr. Fitzgerald.

RODDY. These people who were here before—you mean they— (*Lightly.*) "fancied" or "imagined" experiences, don't you?

PAM. Wouldn't be hard to do at Cliff End. An isolated house, close to the sound of the sea, wind rushing over the moors. (*Irritated with the way they've received the news, Commander Brooke taps his cane on the floor for attention.*)

COMMANDER BROOKE. I felt it was my duty to mention it.

PAM. As long as what they experienced wasn't rats.

COMMANDER BROOKE. (*Decisive.*) It was not rats.

PAM. Are you trying to say they thought the house was possessed in some way?

COMMANDER BROOKE. I have no idea what they thought. As I have said, I felt obliged to mention it.

15

RODDY. Ghosts, eh? A story like that will be quite an attraction to my sister and our friends.

COMMANDER BROOKE. Indeed.

PAM. Perhaps Stella could stop by tomorrow. I have so many questions about the house.

COMMANDER BROOKE. I cannot spare Stella tomorrow. Until this evening—about eight?

PAM. We'll look forward to it. (*Commander Brooke moves to the French doors.*)

RODDY. I'll walk you to the gate, Commander.

COMMANDER BROOKE. There's no need. (*Commander Brooke exits* L. *Roddy moves to the French doors, looks after him.*)

PAM. (*Delighted.*) The house is ours, Roddy. (*Sits on sofa.*) Or soon will be. Aren't you excited?

RODDY. What do you make of the Commander?

PAM. He's a classic curmudgeon.

RODDY. And a stubborn old ram, in the bargain. I shouldn't think anyone has stood up to him in five generations.

PAM. He's certainly rude to that enchanting child. (*Roddy moves back into the room.*)

RODDY. Child? You mean Stella? She's eighteen. You could be her sister.

PAM. She doesn't look eighteen and she doesn't act it. She's not permitted to grow up. She hasn't realized it yet. Something will happen when she does. Commander Brooke doesn't know it, but he's stunting her, spoiling her spontaneity.

RODDY. I admire him for telling us about the "disturbances."

PAM. We probably could have gotten Cliff End for less. I think he wants to get rid of the place.

RODDY. He's honest. He didn't have to tell us about—"ghosts."

PAM. He didn't actually say "ghosts."

RODDY. What else could he have meant? (*Remembers.*) Oh?

PAM. What?

RODDY. We have another mystery. (*Moves* D. L.) A locked room.

PAM. I'll ask Stella for the key.

RODDY. The Commander said Stella doesn't have the key.

PAM. I wonder what it was used for? (*Pam looks about as if she expected to find something near, shivers.*) Oooooh. It is getting chilly in here.

16

RODDY. Nonsense. It's downright toasty. You do have a funny look on your face.

PAM. Then laugh. (*Rubs her arms.*) The strangest sensation. Aren't you cold?

RODDY. Not in the least. Probably dampness. I'm afraid I'm going to have to agree with the old man about Stella's scent. (*Sniffs.*) It's overpowering. Strong, flowery. What did he call it?

PAM. *Mimosa.* I barely noticed it when Stella was in the room.

RODDY. (*Steps behind* D. L. C. *chair.*) We may have gotten more than we bargained for. Cliff End—complete with mysterious memories and a locked room. (*Fakes a sinister tone.*) Maybe tonight spirits will walk.

PAM. That won't bother us.

RODDY. Why not?

PAM. We'll be at the inn. (*Shivers again.*) I'm going to get a jacket. (*Stands.*) I'm positively freezing. (*Pam moves* R.)

RODDY. I'd better have a look at the garage. I hope Commander Brooke has a decent cook. I'm famished already. I wonder if Stella is the chef?

PAM. (*Softly, after a moment's pause.*) That's odd.

RODDY. What is?

PAM. It's not the least bit cold over here.

RODDY. What did I tell you—dampness. Dry rot in the floor under the sofa. The whole house is undoubtedly riddled with drafts from the sea. We'll be lucky if we don't both come down with pneumonia.

PAM. It wasn't that kind of cold. I've never felt anything quite like it.

RODDY. You're quick on the uptake, Pam. The Commander's little story has gotten to you.

PAM. What are you talking about?

RODDY. The cold. Maybe it's spirit mischief.

PAM. You shouldn't take things like that so lightly. Anyway, if spirits walk, it's in places that they've loved. That's why it seems foolish for people to be afraid of them. (*Roddy rubs his hands together in almost boyish relish.*)

RODDY. For my part, I'm delighted. We couldn't have done better if we had to advertise for a haunted house. (*Sound of sea birds up.*)

FAST CURTAIN

ACT I

SCENE 2

Some weeks later. Lizzie Flynn, wearing an apron, is on her knees behind the sofa.

LIZZIE. Her^e, Whiskey. Come along, boy. *(She stands, sighs wearily, rubs her back.)* I don't know where he's got to. *(Crosses* D. L. C., *moves the chair.)* Here, Whiskey. Here, kitty-kitty-kitty. *(Lizzie is middle-aged, outspoken, terribly opinionated, superstitious, but capable and genuinely fond of Roddy and Pam.)* Never knew him to run off before. *(Folds her arms in a defiant gesture.)* Can't say I blame him. *(Pam enters* R. *She wears a smock and carries swatches of fabric, moves to sofa and begins to see which swatch would be best for new upholstery.)*
PAM. Roddy's studio isn't papered yet. The plaster's too bad to take paint. And we'll have to shut up the dining room for the present. It's an arrogant room, difficult to decorate. It will have to wait till we're rich, I'm afraid. *(Another swatch.)* Do you think this might do? *(Lizzie doesn't answer.)* Lizzie? *(Pam looks up.)* What's wrong?
LIZZIE. He's gone again.
PAM. What are you talking about?
LIZZIE. Whiskey. He don't like this house, Miss Pamela. Cats are very perceptive.
PAM. Don't start that nonsense again. I never should have told you what Commander Brooke said about the previous tenants. *(Pam sits on sofa, places fabric swatches on the table, arranges them for appraisal.)*
LIZZIE. *(Steps behind* D. R. C. *chair.)* What do I care about previous tenants? I can sense things for myself.
PAM. Lizzie Flynn, you're incorrigible. You have three vices—gossip, superstition and Whiskey.
LIZZIE. I wish you wouldn't say it like that. Whiskey, I mean. Anyone would think you meant liquor instead of a cat.
PAM. You must admit it's an odd name for a cat.
LIZZIE. It's a perfect name for a cat. He whisks his tail side to side, don't he?
PAM. He's probably found romance in the neighborhood.

18

LIZZIE. Lot of good it'll do him. The vet's had a go at him, you know.

PAM. Sit down and help me decide. (*Lizzie sits. Pam points to the fabric samples as she speaks.*) This might do for curtains in the master bedroom . . . and this might work nicely in the sewing room. I must stop saying sewing room. It's now Roddy's study.

LIZZIE. He won't go upstairs— (*Points to nursery door.*) and as far as that room is concerned, he'll have none of it.

PAM. What on earth are you talking about?

LIZZIE. Whiskey, of course.

PAM. Back to that. You're trying to say that Whiskey has seen something out of the ordinary, is that it?

LIZZIE. Whiskey can purr for himself. (*Pause.*) I only know what *I* saw. (*Lizzie has spoken "I only know what I saw" with such seriousness that Pam is startled.*)

PAM. When?

LIZZIE. Last evening. After you and Mr. Roddy went into the village for your game of darts.

PAM. (*Pointedly.*) Tell me quite clearly what you saw.

LIZZIE. (*Hesitates.*) I don't like to be laughed at.

PAM. No one will laugh at you.

LIZZIE. (*Disturbed.*) 'Twill be carved on my heart till my dying day.

PAM. (*Annoyed.*) *What* will?

LIZZIE. In the hall, I was, locking the door. The top bolt's a bit high for me; I had to get up on a chair— (*The recollection is unnerving for Lizzie. She stands, grabs the back of her chair for courage.*)

PAM. Go on—

LIZZIE. 'Twas Whiskey I noticed first. I heard a fierce growl from h:m, and heaven shield us, there he was under the hall chest flattened to the floor with terror, his two eyes glaring like lamps and his teeth savage— It was a lady, Miss Pamela. I screamed like mad, because it gave me such a fright to see anybody, thinking I was in the house alone, but I thought at first she was as real as you or I. Standing there, leaning over the banister, she was, just as you might yourself, and staring down into the hall. All in white, she was, with long fair hair. But oh, pitiful saints, the awful look in her eyes.

PAM. What kind of a look was it?

19

LIZZIE. Don't ask me. I want to forget.

PAM. (*Demands.*) Lizzie.

LIZZIE. Blue her eyes were, and terrible, as if she was looking down into hell. By the blue eyes I could tell it was the lady who was killed on the cliff. It went through me like a blast of ice. I never was so cold. Then, in a wink, she was gone. (*Pam moves to her, speaks comfortingly.*)

PAM. Poor Lizzie. Why didn't you say something at breakfast?

LIZZIE. And have Mr. Roddy grinning like a schoolboy? Besides, I was too scared to speak about it. I got up and went to early Mass and I had a lovely talk with the priest. He's a grand, wise man, is Father Anson—he says I'm not to stay alone in this house again. (*Roddy enters* R., *wearing a jacket and carrying a manuscript.*)

RODDY. I put your things in the car, Pam. Come on, out of your smock. I want to get started. (*Holds up manuscript.*) I finished the first draft. Still doesn't feel right. (*Sees the grave expressions on Pam and Lizzie.*) I've seen happier faces on labels advertising vinegar. (*The remark snaps Lizzie out of her mood.*)

LIZZIE. You have much to answer for, Mr. Roddy. Bringing a decent woman like myself to a place like this. (*To Pam.*) Maybe he's down by the potting shed. (*She exits* L. *Roddy sits on sofa.*)

RODDY. Who's down by the potting shed?

PAM. (*Distracted.*) Whiskey's run off again.

RODDY. After field mice.

PAM. That's not what Lizzie thinks.

RODDY. (*Flipping pages of his manuscript.*) I suppose I could take this first draft to Max. He's got a good sense of what works and what doesn't. Get his opinion. Stella's read a couple scenes. We had a long walk on the beach yesterday.

PAM. Lizzie has seen a ghost.

RODDY. I'm afraid that's some of my doing. She *is* gullible and *wholly* Irish. We're only *half* Irish, thankfully.

PAM. You mean we're only entitled to see half a ghost? The poor thing was in a state.

RODDY. I do tease her. It's hard to resist. You don't meet too many people these days who still believe in leprechauns. (*Pam moves into the hallway,* R., *taking off her smock as she crosses.*)

PAM. You mustn't do it anymore. Mrs. Jessup fills her head with all sorts of foolishness about the house, as it is.

RODDY. Where did she see this "apparition"?

PAM. (*Offstage.*) On the stairs. She says, by the blue eyes, it was the lady who was killed on the cliff. All in white, long fair hair.

RODDY. Rather a romantic description of a ghost. Conventional, too. (*Pam returns. She has taken off the smock and carries a light coat over one arm.*)

PAM. Do try to be serious for a moment. (*Tentative.*) You don't think there's anything to it? (*She moves L. of sofa, puts down coat.*)

RODDY. Lizzie *wanted* to see a ghost. Living here, she'd lose prestige with Mrs. Jessup if she failed to see something.

PAM. (*Looks U. C.*) Her description is very much like the portrait.

RODDY. Precisely. There you have it. The power of autosuggestion.

PAM. She was so upset. That's not like Lizzie.

RODDY. She's heard Mary Meredith described. She's heard about the accident on the cliff and she sees the portrait every day. Her reaction is understandable.

PAM. Why are you so skeptical?

RODDY. The more you expect something, the more you get attuned to it and the more you subject yourself to obsession. I'm not entirely skeptical. I think there *is* something psychic in the place.

PAM. If Mary Meredith haunts this house, there must be a reason.

RODDY. You're doing exactly what Lizzie did—setting yourself up to see something that isn't there.

PAM. The previous tenants experienced "something." Commander Brooke told us that.

RODDY. You mean the Parkinsons. I had a long talk with Dr. Scott in the village. Those "disturbances" were apparently invented as an excuse to break their lease. They went off without paying their debts.

PAM. But that awful cold that comes and goes. It makes me quite depressed.

RODDY. The house is drafty.

PAM. There's something else. (*Moves toward nursery door.*) I didn't want to worry you. I thought, perhaps, it wouldn't come back, but it does. At night. (*Roddy slams down his manuscript, annoyed.*) It comes from the nursery. (*Gestures to the door.*) A heartbreaking sound, like someone weeping.

RODDY. Birds in the chimney, or mice, or a bat, wind.

21

PAM. I can see you're in no mood to humor me.

RODDY. Why do you suppose the nursery was so far from the other bedrooms?

PAM. Perhaps Stella could tell you. It was her nursery. She rang up this morning. I told her we were off for a little holiday. Poor thing—Commander's in the hospital for tests.

RODDY. I must show you something I found when I was cleaning out the nursery. (*He crosses to the nursery, enters, leaves door open.*)

PAM. (*Calls in.*) Odd the way the Commander left everything for us, the good and the bad, some really fine pieces and some junk.

RODDY. (*Offstage.*) What do you make of this?

PAM. I'll know when I see what it is. (*He returns, carrying a wooden chest, puts it down. He kneels behind it, D. L. Pam moves close.*)

RODDY. (*Opens lid.*) I suppose these were Llewellyn's props. (*Takes out a fringed shawl.*) It's escaped the moths.

PAM. (*Takes it, opens it.*) It's pretty.

RODDY. (*Takes out a fan.*) This, too.

PAM. (*Takes it, spreads it.*) What else is in there?

RODDY. (*Rummages.*) Some combs, artificial flowers, a pair of castanets, things like that. (*Pulls out a small phial or bottle.*) And this.

PAM. (*Takes it.*) Perfume flask. There's an initial on it . . . "G." And some writing I can't make out.

RODDY. Ancient by the looks of it.

PAM. (*Removes stopper, sniffs.*) Not even a whisper left.

RODDY. Here's the *real* treasure. (*He takes a rolled-up canvas from the chest.*) Look at this. (*He moves D. L. C., sits, unrolls canvas on side table. Pam joins him.*)

PAM. A poster of some sort?

RODDY. Hardly.

PAM. (*Looks.*) It's a painting.

RODDY. Some of Meredith's work would be my guess.

PAM. It's a preliminary study by the looks of it, quite detailed.

RODDY. I believe I've seen the finished painting, but I can't remember where.

PAM. The Commander takes a dim view of his son-in-law. I do think Stella should have her father's work, but I don't know what her grandfather would say.

22

RODDY. You know what he'd say.
PAM. I don't care for this at all.
RODDY. It's cleverly done.
PAM. A young girl and an old woman.
RODDY. You're missing the point.
PAM. How so?
RODDY. Look again.
PAM. (*Looks, holds it up.*) It's not an old woman, is it? The face
is young but gaunt, haggard. A hideous caricature.
RODDY. Yes, a hideous caricature. But the two women in this
painting are the same person. It's an *unmerciful* study in decay.
PAM. (*Rolls it up.*) I don't care to have this up on a wall.
RODDY. You have gotten yourself in a mood and I know the
thing to snap you out of it. (*Pam returns the rolled-up canvas to
the chest, shuts lid.*)
PAM. Bristol.
RODDY. No, not Bristol—a housewarming.
PAM. *Housewarming?* (*Excitedly.*) That is a wonderful idea!
(*Thinks.*) It's out of the question.
RODDY. Why?
PAM. Nothing's ready. The rooms are unfinished, all the curtains
haven't come, no carpeting on the stairs—
RODDY. All the more reason to go ahead with the suggestion.
We'll make do with what we have. Nothing extravagant. We'll
ask Max and Wendy. (*Pam throws off her previous depression,
gets caught up in the idea of a housewarming.*)
PAM. I'll see what I can find in Bristol in the morning. They have
some good shops.
RODDY. Good. That's settled. A housewarming, it is.
MRS. JESSUP. (*Offstage.*) 'Allo.
RODDY. Who's that? (*Pam moves to French doors.*)
PAM. It's Mrs. Jessup.
RODDY. (*Stands.*) Careful what you say. She's a snoop. (*He
crosses to chest, picks it up, enters nursery.*)
PAM. That chest is quite handsome. I'll find a place for it. (*Calls
out.*) Do come in, Mrs. Jessup. (*Mrs. Jessup enters. She's a small
and alert country woman wearing a rather comical hat and carry-
ing a covered basket on her arm.*)
MRS. JESSUP. The wind's coming up. Your wicker lawn furniture
will have a toss.

23

PAM. That's one old chair and a bench. Rickety stuff it is, too.

MRS. JESSUP. 'Tis a real comfort to have neighbors again.

PAM. Sit down, Mrs. Jessup.

MRS. JESSUP. Don't mind if I do. (*She crosses to sofa and sits, perfectly at home. Roddy returns, closes nursery door.*) Came by to pick up your Lizzie.

PAM. She's going into the village?

MRS. JESSUP. Says she's spending the night with me and my Charlie since you and your brother are off to the city and won't be back 'til morning.

RODDY. She never said a word to me.

PAM. Nor to me.

MRS. JESSUP. I saw her in the village this morning. She had plenty to say, then. (*Pam and Roddy nod to each other. Just as they figured—gossip.*) So nice that you're not at all like the Parkinsons. I never cared for them, with their great dogs chasing the sheep and never paying me what they owed for— (*Holds up basket.*) eggs and such. Unchristian it may be, but I blessed whatever it was chased them out of Cliff End. Whatever it was it certainly wasn't the gentle soul that's gone.

PAM. The Commander's daughter?

MRS. JESSUP. Ay, his only child. She wouldn't hurt her worst enemy, would Mary Meredith. Threw her life away, striving to save that wildcat, Carmel. That what most believe. (*Mrs. Jessup is perfectly aware she's tossed out bait.*)

RODDY. (*Moves c.*) Carmel?

MRS. JESSUP. Supposed to be a sort of lady's maid to Mrs. Meredith. They brought her back from foreign parts. Spain. Wild as a gypsy in her ways. Crazy, too. Always threatening to throw herself off the cliff.

RODDY. Is that how it happened? The accident on the cliff?

MRS. JESSUP. No living soul knows what happened, Mr. Fitzgerald, or ever will know—unless—I don't like to talk out of turn, you understand. I don't approve of gossip.

RODDY. (*Urging her on.*) Neither do we. (*Quickly.*) Unless what—

MRS. JESSUP. Not what—who. Miss Holloway.

PAM. (*Sits D. L. C.*) Who's Miss Holloway? (*Mrs. Jessup enjoys an audience for her sensational rumors.*)

24

MRS. JESSUP. The nurse. If you ask me, Miss Holloway knew more than she'd say. (*Lizzie enters* R., *coat and hat on.*)

LIZZIE. Ready when you are, Mrs. Jessup.

PAM. You might have told us you were spending the night away from Cliff End.

LIZZIE. I told you what Father Anson said.

MRS. JESSUP. The Parkinsons' cook saw a ghost. Fainted dead away, she did. (*To Pam, hopeful.*) Have you experienced any "disturbances," Miss Fitzgerald? Anything unusual you might like to tell me about? Anything at all?

RODDY. (*Eager to get the whole story.*) What did the nurse say?

MRS. JESSUP. There was a storm. Said she saw Mary Meredith and Carmel at the edge of the cliff. Carmel was running and Mrs. Meredith after her. It was as if the wind took Carmel and flung her into the tree: she could see her, in her black dress clinging to it. Mary Meredith couldn't stop herself on the slope. Mary flung herself sideways, making a grab at the tree, but she fell back and went down. That's what Miss Holloway said.

PAM. Was Mary Meredith killed instantly?

MRS. JESSUP. Broke her back, poor lady; not a scar on her lovely face, but a bruise, they did say, on the side of her head. It broke her father's heart.

LIZZIE. (*Steps* R. *of sofa.*) Poor old man.

RODDY. And the girl she was trying to save?

PAM. Carmel—she was all right?

MRS. JESSUP. Not for long. In a week she was dead in her bed in this very house.

LIZZIE. (*Aghast.*) You never told me Carmel died in this house.

MRS. JESSUP. I don't like to tell tales. It was none of my business. To each his own, I always say.

PAM. How did Carmel die?

MRS. JESSUP. (*With relish.*) Ran off, that night, in the storm, no one knew where. They found her two days later, sick and raving, up in Hartley's barn. Old Mrs. Hartley was afraid to take her in, so they put her on a farm cart and brought her home. She died in Miss Holloway's arms.

RODDY. And Llewellyn Meredith? What happened to him?

MRS. JESSUP. (*Distastefully.*) Him? (*Delighted to cut him down.*) There were no tears shed in Biddlecombe for him. He had no heart to break! Finished up his work, took himself off abroad.

The village heard nothing of him for three years, when news came that the ocean swallowed him up. The fishes needed a dose of salts when they got done with Mr. Meredith. *(Her mood shifts, pleasant as can be, she stands.)* Shall I have Charlie bring by fresh eggs in the morning?

LIZZIE. I'll carry them back myself.

MRS. JESSUP. *(Moves R.)* Aren't you going to bring the cat? I brought along this basket for him.

LIZZIE. *(An incriminating look to Pam and Roddy.)* Couldn't find him.

MRS. JESSUP. Come along, dear. Car's out front. Goodbye all. *(She exits R., followed by Lizzie.)*

PAM AND RODDY. Goodbye, Mrs. Jessup.

LIZZIE. Mind you, lock the front door, Mr. Roddy. *(She's out. Pam and Roddy don't know quite what to say, then:)*

PAM. I've heard bits and pieces of the story in the village, but Mrs. Jessup does have a way of filling in the holes.

RODDY. I doubt it. She enjoys an audience and plays to it. I wouldn't trust her memory, either. That was fifteen years ago. You saw how she was trying to scratch up something more recent.

PAM. Be a lamb and close the drapes. *(Pam stands, puts on her coat. Roddy crosses L., pulls drapes across the French doors plunging the room into shadows. Pam shivers.)* There it is again.

RODDY. What?

PAM. That cold—that terrible cold.

RODDY. There's a wind storm blowing up.

PAM. I don't like it, Roddy. *(Rubs her arms.)* I don't like it at all.

RODDY. *(He crosses down to her.)* We both can do with a change. Bristol it is, and a very fine dinner in a very fine restaurant. *(Pam smiles at him, grateful for his good sense. They exit R. Sound of wind up. A moment passes, the wind dies down. Sound of front door closing, offstage. A melody floats on the stillness of the room—eerie, slightly atonal, unnerving. The portrait of Mary Meredith begins to glow (consult production notes) barely noticeable at first—as if a silvery mist were gathering. There is motion at the drapes. Someone has opened the French doors. A moment passes and Stella enters the room surreptitiously. The glow on the portrait and the melody fade away. Stella hasn't noticed. She moves R., stands by the entry, looks offstage, ascer-*

taining that she's alone in the house. Suddenly, from behind the nursery door comes the sound of a woman weeping—forlorn, tragic, lonely. Stella turns. She is not afraid. Sound of music box. She moves C., her attention on the door. It slowly opens . . . A bluish light, like the spill from a night light or a baby's lamp, comes from the room's interior. Sound of weeping is louder. Stella speaks warmly, lovingly:)

STELLA. There's no need to cry, Mother . . . I'm here . . . I'm here . . . *(Stella moves to the nursery, her arms outstretched to embrace something, as yet, unseen. Outside Cliff End, the wind howls.)*

CURTAIN

END OF ACT I

ACT II

SCENE 1

Two weeks later, the housewarming. Evening. The sitting room is attractively lighted and flowers have been placed about to give a festive note. A fire glows in the hearth. The wooden chest has been placed by the nursery door as a decorative touch. The shawl covers it. A radio or stereo has been added and a few seconds prior to curtain, we hear background music, unobtrusive, soft, listenable.

Wendy, a vivacious young actress, sits on the sofa, Pam beside her. Roddy sits D. R. C. Max Hilliard, a painter, about Roddy's age, stands by the French doors, holding a glass of wine. The drapes are drawn apart. Other glasses are on the table in front of sofa, along with some tarot cards that Wendy has been reading. Roddy and Wendy are laughing good-naturedly.

WENDY. *(Holds up a tarot card.)* No, no, it's perfectly true. You can learn much about yourself, past, present and future, if you pay attention to the tarot cards.

MAX. It's something like parlor magic.

WENDY. Not in the least like parlor magic.

PAM. I thought you gave me an excellent reading.

WENDY. There! You hear, Max?

MAX. It's not cricket. You know Pam's temperament already.

WENDY. What has that to do with anything?

MAX. That colors the reading.

WENDY. It does no such thing.

MAX. I must admit that Wendy's quite knowledgeable about this sort of thing. *(Wendy shuffles the tarot cards, cuts them, begins to set them out.)*

WENDY. I'm glad you appreciate my gift, Max. Anyone can be an actress, but it takes *genuine* talent to read the tarot cards.

RODDY. I wish Stella could have a reading.

PAM. Roddy's become fond of the young woman who used to own this house.

WENDY. I hope you haven't been leading us on.

PAM. In what way?

WENDY. Your ghost. I've never encountered a ghost and I've been in some of the grand old houses—now that I'm here in Cliff End perhaps I'll get lucky. Witness a manifestation. That's the dream of every psychic. This place is an open invitation to ghosts.

RODDY. What makes you say that?

WENDY. The features of the house. Set back from a cliff, that long stairway, the many little rooms, the faraway neighbors. (*Lizzie enters* R. *She wears a dark dress and starched apron. She holds a plate of appetizers, moves in front of sofa. Max looks into the night.*)

MAX. I can see a car pulling in.

PAM. That'll be Dr. Scott. I want you to meet him. He knows more about the village than anyone.

WENDY. The house needs more mirrors. Ghosts hate mirrors. They're terrified by their own reflections. A mirror on every wall would be ghost-proof.

LIZZIE. (*Disapproves of the conversation.*) Fishy.

RODDY. What's that, Lizzie?

LIZZIE. The appetizers. They're fishy.

PAM. Put the plate down, Lizzie, and see to Dr. Scott.

LIZZIE. (*Puts down the plate, points to cards.*) What are those things?

WENDY. Tarot cards.

LIZZIE. I thought as much.

WENDY. Would you like me to read them for you? (*Lizzie moves* R.)

LIZZIE. (*Outraged.*) I would not! I don't approve of that sort of thing. There's enough that goes on in this house without inviting more, fooling with things we ought to leave alone. (*She exits.*)

MAX. (*Turns.*) So much for Lizzie and tarot cards. She tells me she's actually seen something.

RODDY. She'd like to be one up on our neighbor, Mrs. Jessup, and tell her she spent one night here alone, but so far she hasn't been able to summon up the courage.

29

WENDY. (*Returns the cards to their box.*) Do tell us all about your play, Roddy.

MAX. (*Turns.*) There's speculation about it. I've seen mention of it in a column or two. (*Pam stands, crosses to radio, snaps it off.*)

PAM. That's one reason we got out of London. Roddy had to work away from pressure and distraction.

MAX. At least in my profession, I can sell a canvas before a critic is able to tell a prospective buyer it's not worth the price. I do admire your sense of adventure. When a literary critic decides to write a play he temps the fates. You could be calling down fire and brimstone on your head.

WENDY. I hope there's a marvellous part in it for me. I'm playing Bristol in a few weeks.

RODDY. We shall be there on opening night.

PAM. I'm hoping Roddy will read his play to you.

RODDY. I'd welcome comments.

MAX. Splendid. You'll get them.

WENDY. What do you call the play?

RODDY. *Barbara.*

WENDY. (*Frowns.*) Doesn't grab. I'd work on a new title.

RODDY. A negative review for the title? The future does not look promising.

WENDY. Never mind the title. What's the play about?

RODDY. It's a psychological crime play—

WENDY. —I like it already—

RODDY. —a melodrama rooted in character; a thriller, true to life. It's got everything: original characters, nice, dry, ironic humor, juicy dialogue, and plot.

WENDY. Modesty was never one of your virtues, Roddy, and I'm glad of it. I can't abide humility. Thrillers are all the rage now. You can make your reputation in London, but New York's the place to go for money.

MAX. I forgot.

RODDY. What?

MAX. You know that preliminary sketch you described on the phone, the one by Llewellyn Meredith?

WENDY. What has that to do with Roddy's play?

MAX. As far as I know, absolutely nothing.

PAM. You've tracked it down?

30

MAX. Better than that. I have a good reproduction in one of the books I brought along.

RODDY. I'll want to see that. (*Lizzie appears* R.)

LIZZIE. Dr. Scott's here, Miss Pamela. (*Dr. Scott enters. He's a likeable middle-aged man who makes friends easily.*)

MAX. Lizzie, be a good soul and get that large book you'll find on my night table.

LIZZIE. (*Sour.*) They've been fooling with tarot cards, Dr. Scott. (*She exits. Pam crosses to him, takes his arm. Roddy stands.*)

PAM. I'm so glad you were able to make it.

DR. SCOTT. I've been hinting for a dinner invitation ever since you opened the house.

PAM. I want you to meet two of our dearest friends. Wendy Carey and Max Hilliard.

WENDY. How are you, Doctor?

DR. SCOTT. A doctor is always fine, Miss Carey. Anything less would be bad public relations. (*Max crosses to him, they shake hands.*)

MAX. I'm going to paint the landscape. I'll want to have a chat with you. I like to get the feel of a place. I understand you know all about Biddlecombe.

DR. SCOTT. There's not much to know, is there?

RODDY. Sit down, Dr. Scott. (*He sits on sofa, beside Wendy. Roddy sits.*)

PAM. (*To Max.*) I did want you and Wendy to meet Stella and her grandfather, but the old Commander has no love for this house and he's all but forbidden Stella to visit.

WENDY. (*Excited.*) Do you believe in exorcism, Dr. Scott? (*He's astonished by her question.*)

DR. SCOTT. Good heavens. (*Max moves* U. C., *studies portrait. Pam crosses* D. C.)

RODDY. I take it Lizzie has told you about the resident ghost.

DR. SCOTT. To be precise, it was Mrs. Jessup who spread the alarm.

PAM. That figures. May I get you a glass of wine, Doctor?

DR. SCOTT. A glass at dinner is all I allow myself. Father Anson is concerned. He's afraid you may find that you can't live in this house.

MAX. If there is a ghost disturbing things, surely something can be done.

31

WENDY. My point exactly—exorcism.

PAM. (Sits D. L. C.) Don't you think that it might be possible to do something less drastic that would give the troubled spirit rest?

DR. SCOTT. First you'd have to discover who the ghost is.

(Roddy crosses to portrait.)

RODDY. I'd say that was obvious. Mary Meredith.

WENDY. Not necessarily. You said five generations have lived in this house. The ghost could be from the far past. (Caught up in the topic.) Did she really die by accident?

PAM. We understand that there was a doubt in Miss Holloway's mind.

WENDY. Do you think it's possible that the girl—Carmel—struck her?

DR. SCOTT. It's not likely, but, at such a moment of terror, not impossible, perhaps.

MAX. She was Meredith's model?

DR. SCOTT. Yes. She was a dancer, I understand. Posed for him in Spain.

PAM. That was before his marriage, of course?

DR. SCOTT. Just before. That was the time when he and Mary met. She was wintering for her health in Seville. After the marriage she insisted on returning to England. She was devoted to her father and wouldn't leave him alone. The Commander gave them this house.

RODDY. And they brought Carmel back with them?

DR. SCOTT. From what I've been told—village whispers—Meredith insisted that he couldn't lose his model, and Mary—well, great kindness isn't always accompanied by wisdom. Mary loved doing a generous thing. (Lizzie enters R., carrying a large art book. Max motions her to him. He takes the book.)

WENDY. Was she—Carmel—here for long?

DR. SCOTT. Perhaps six months. Then, in the winter, they all went abroad. Mary was delicate and our winters are harsh. In the spring they returned—Meredith, that is, and Mary and their baby, who was born in France.

RODDY. Stella?

DR. SCOTT. Yes. Meredith was devoted to her—his saving grace. (Lizzie crosses behind sofa; Max flips the pages of the book.)

32

LIZZIE. (*Looks at plate.*) No sense bringing in another plate when you haven't eaten what I brought in the last time.

PAM. How is dinner coming along?

LIZZIE. Half an hour should do it. You know, I don't like to be rushed, Miss Pam. (*Lizzie exits* R.)

PAM. Ever since Whiskey ran off, Lizzie's been short-tempered.

DR. SCOTT. Whiskey?

WENDY. Her cat.

DR. SCOTT. Curious name for a cat.

WENDY. What became of Carmel?

DR. SCOTT. She got a position in Paris, I believe. A fashion model. Then, sometime later, she returned here to Cliff End. (*Max has found something in the book.*)

MAX. Here it is! I'll give you odds, this is a portrait of Carmel. (*All look to Max. Roddy takes the book, moves* D.)

RODDY. This is the painting, Pam. I knew I had seen it someplace.

MAX. The Lyndon Gallery in London. (*Roddy shows the page to Pam. Max moves* L. *of Pam.*) It's called *The Artist's Model.* Caused something of a stir when it first appeared fifteen years ago.

PAM. I think it's monstrous, to record a woman's decline so cruelly.

DR. SCOTT. May I have a look? (*Roddy hands him the book. Wendy looks over Dr. Scott's shoulder.*)

MAX. The young woman is a beauty, if you like that type.

WENDY. Bright eyes, a pretty smile.

DR. SCOTT. Yes, I believe this is Carmel.

RODDY. Couldn't be anyone else.

WENDY. I see what you mean, Pam. He's painted her young and beautiful and, then, with her beauty gone. How tragic, how sad. I hope she never saw this painting.

MAX. How could she miss not seeing it? She posed for it.

PAM. Dr. Scott, were you with Carmel when she died?

DR. SCOTT. No. Nurse Holloway was in charge.

RODDY. I'd like to have a talk with that woman. Do you know where we might find her?

DR. SCOTT. She runs a spa of sorts out from Bristol. A "Center of Healing through Harmony."

WENDY. Sounds like a nudist colony.

DR. SCOTT. I'm told she does quite well. I don't pretend to understand her methods, but I gather her treatment combines diet with healthy thoughts.

RODDY. I wonder if she'll see me.

DR. SCOTT. She's not an approachable woman. I had differences with her. At one time I thought of bringing her up on charges. I wasn't satisfied with the way she handled her patient.

PAM. You mean Carmel?

DR. SCOTT. (Nods.) I felt this house had already seen enough trouble.

PAM. Let's change the subject. This is supposed to be a happy occasion. (Wendy stiffens with fright.)

WENDY. Listen.

MAX. To what? (All listen.) I don't hear anything.

WENDY. Strange—

DR. SCOTT. What is it, Miss Carey?

WENDY. I could have sworn I heard someone—"weeping." (Roddy and Pam look fearful.)

RODDY. Probably Lizzie. From the kitchen.

WENDY. No—in here—there it is again. (All strain to listen. Nothing for a moment and, then, barely audible, from the nursery comes the sound of a woman softly weeping. Wendy stands, points.) There—behind that door—someone's in there. You heard it, didn't you, Dr. Scott?

DR. SCOTT. (Uncertain.) I'm not sure—

MAX. I think I heard something, but I can't be sure, either.

WENDY. (Emotional.) Listen— (Again, all tense. Sound of music box—vague, tinkly, distant.)

MAX. (Incredulous.) Music. (Confirms.) It's music.

RODDY. I don't think so.

MAX. (Insists.) Music, I tell you. A music box. (The melody fades as weakly and as strangely as it arrived.)

WENDY. Who is it in there?

RODDY. I don't know, but I intend to find out.

PAM. (Stands.) Be careful, Roddy. (Max stands to one side as Roddy moves to the nursery door, hesitates for a moment, opens it, enters. No one moves, their attention focused D. L. The melody we heard at the conclusion of Act 1 returns—eerie, atonal, unnerving. The portrait of Mary Meredith begins to glow. Wendy experiences a chill, rubs her arms.)

WENDY. Oh!

34

DR. SCOTT. What is it?

WENDY. It's so cold, so terribly cold.

PAM. (*Worried, calls to nursery.*) Roddy, are you all right?

MAX. You wished a little too hard for a ghost, Wendy.

WENDY. Aren't you cold?

MAX. (*Shivers.*) Yes, I am. Strange sensation. I'm cold, yet I don't know why. The room's warm enough.

PAM. (*Very nervous.*) Roddy, what is it? (*Long pause. Roddy returns and the glow on the portrait fades, the melody is heard no more.*)

RODDY. There's no one in there.

WENDY. We *heard* someone.

DR. SCOTT. The wind can play tricks.

WENDY. It was a woman sobbing.

MAX. The music—we heard a music box.

RODDY. No, I don't think so. There's a wind chime outside the nursery window. The window was open at the top. I've closed it.

PAM. I've heard the crying before, Wendy. You didn't imagine it.

WENDY. I know what you mean about the cold. I was freezing.

DR. SCOTT. So was I. A peculiar sensation. It went as quickly as it came. (*Stella, dressed charmingly, enters* R.)

STELLA. I didn't mean to keep you waiting. (*All turn.*)

PAM. Stella! How did you manage it?

DR. SCOTT. I brought Stella along.

STELLA. I had to visit my mother's room once more. I should have come in right away, but I was too excited. (*Pam crosses to her, motions others to be silent about what's happened by putting a finger to her lips.*)

RODDY. We're delighted. (*Stella smiles at him. It's plain they've come to enjoy each other's company.*)

STELLA. The house is lovelier than I could have imagined. You've done so much with it.

PAM. Not nearly enough. Give us time. (*Pam guides her into the room.*) This is Max Hilliard, a fine painter.

MAX. Delighted to meet you, Miss Meredith.

PAM. Wendy Carey.

STELLA. Hello.

WENDY. Hello.

PAM. She'll be playing in Bristol in a few weeks. Roddy and I are going to see her play. Maybe you could come with us.

STELLA. I'd have to ask Grandfather's permission.

RODDY. (*Steps to* D. L. C. *chair.*) Sit here, Stella. (*She crosses to chair. Wendy sits.*)

STELLA I am glad I was able to come this evening.

RODDY. I'm still trying to figure out how you got away.

STELLA. (*Sits.*) I have Dr. Scott to thank for it. He made Grandfather think it would be unfair not to let me come, and Grandfather is never unfair. (*Stella smiles sweetly, but realizes from the expressions that something is amiss.*) Is something wrong? (*They look at each other, not wanting to discuss what happened in front of Stella.*)

DR. SCOTT. (*Thinking fast.*) We were just admiring some of your father's work. (*He holds up book.*)

STELLA. I wish I knew more about him. Grandfather has never talked about him, nor has Miss Holloway. They disliked him, I'm afraid.

RODDY. Were you fond of this Miss Holloway?

STELLA. She was Mother's devoted friend. I wasn't a lovable baby.

WENDY. Who told you such a thing? I never heard of a baby who wasn't lovable.

STELLA. Miss Holloway says I was cross and tiresome and never pretty at all.

MAX. Your Miss Holloway sounds like a perfect witch.

STELLA. She's kind really, in her own way. It's just that it's difficult to feel close to a governess.

WENDY. She was your governess, too?

STELLA. After Mother passed away, yes. (*Looks to painting.*) That's Mother.

MAX. We know. Portrait fits the room.

PAM. We'd gladly give you the portrait, Stella, but the Commander wouldn't approve. If you ever take a place of your own, it's yours.

STELLA. You are good friends. (*Looks to fireplace.*) I'm afraid the fireplace doesn't throw out much heat.

MAX. You're cold?

STELLA. (*Rubs her arms.*) I wasn't—until a moment ago. (*Others react. Nervously, Wendy takes out a compact, opens it, begins to fluff her hair. The voice is taut, edgy, harsh—a dramatic shift in mood.*)

WENDY. What right did he have to paint a picture like that! To take youth and turn it into something grotesque and corrupted.

MAX. What on earth are you talking about? (*Wendy is clearly not herself, pulls at her hair.*)

WENDY. It was a wicked thing to do! Wicked, wicked. Llewellyn Meredith was a swine! (*Stella is shocked. Max steps toward her. The others are alarmed.*)

MAX. What's wrong with you? (*Wendy looks into the compact mirror, stifles a scream. The compact drops to the table. She dissolves into tears, collapses on the sofa, D. R. Dr. Scott stands, steps behind the sofa. Pam crosses to sofa, sits beside her.*)

DR. SCOTT. What is it, Miss Carey?

PAM. Wendy, what's happened?

WENDY. (*Terrified.*) In the mirror. (*Pam looks to Dr. Scott. He nods that Pam should pick it up. She does, wary.*)

PAM. You saw something in the mirror? (*She nods. Pam looks.*) It's only a mirror. An ordinary compact mirror. What did you see? (*Wendy fights to get control of herself. Max and Roddy move closer. As the scene continues, the glow returns on the portrait, but only Stella notices. She stands, moves U. C. The eerie music underscores.*)

WENDY. (*With difficulty.*) I saw—

MAX. Go on.

WENDY. (*Shaking.*) I saw a death's head. I suddenly looked old. Ghastly. Stark old age. Death's-head old age.

MAX. You could never look like that. (*Dr. Scott puts his hand to her forehead and cheek.*)

DR. SCOTT. She doesn't feel feverish.

PAM. She's had a terrible shock.

DR. SCOTT. I think it would be wise to get her upstairs.

PAM. Yes, by all means. (*Stella stands motionless in front of the portrait. She moves L., opens one of the French doors slightly, exits. No one has noticed. The glow on the portrait and the ghost melody fade.*)

DR. SCOTT. I'll get my bag from the car.

PAM. No need. I'll send Lizzie for it. (*Pam and Dr. Scott help Wendy to her feet, guide her R.*)

WENDY. It's my future, I know it is. That's what the mirror was trying to tell me.

PAM. You'll feel much better once you've rested.

DR. SCOTT. I'll have you back with us in no time. (*They're out. Max picks up the compact mirror, studies his own reflection.*)

MAX. Nothing in the mirror. I'll take this up to her and make her look again.

RODDY. Leave her with the doctor.

MAX. What could have happened to her?

RODDY. I think you're getting an idea of what I've been talking about.

MAX. If this is a sample of what goes on at Cliff End, I think you'd better shut the place up and come back to London. The sooner the better. I've seen people in shock. That's Wendy's condition.

RODDY. Seeing that picture of Meredith's in the book may have planted the seed.

MAX. Wendy is a sane and sensible young woman. I've never known her to go off like that.

RODDY. I'm sorry you had to witness that, Stella. Not what I had planned for our housewarming. (*Only now do they realize Stella is not in the room. They look around.*)

MAX. She was here a moment ago. (*Sees the open French door.*) Out there. She's gone outside. (*Max and Roddy move to the French door, peer out into the night.*) There she goes.

RODDY. Where?

MAX. There! Running across the lawn. (*A warning.*) She's heading for the cliff.

RODDY. Stella! Stella! (*He runs out. Lizzie, excited, enters* R.)

LIZZIE. What is going on?

MAX. Get the doctor's bag and hurry.

LIZZIE. I want to know what's going on.

MAX. (*A command.*) Don't argue! (*He dashes out after Roddy.*)

LIZZIE. I don't take orders from guests. (*She crosses to French doors, looks off. Pamela enters* R.)

PAM. Lizzie, I sent you to Dr. Scott's car. What are you doing in here?

LIZZIE. Never mind what I'm doing in here, Miss Pamela. (*Points, agitated.*) What's she doing out there?

PAM. Who?

LIZZIE. Stella Meredith. (*Frantic, Pam crosses to French doors. Lizzie reacts to the offstage action.*) She's almost to the edge. (*Pam looks, is horrified. Fast, she crosses back across stage.*)

PAM. Dr. Scott! Dr. Scott!

LIZZIE. She's by that evil tree, Miss Pam. She's almost over! (*Pam wheels about, horrified.*)

PAM. No!

LIZZIE. (*Relieved.*) Thank the saints! Mr. Roddy grabbed her in time. A second more and she'd have been ready for judgment. (*Pam is shaken.*)

PAM. I think I'm going to need Dr. Scott for myself. (*She sits on chair near entry, breathes heavily.*) I may faint. (*Lizzie pours a glass of brandy from a decanter, crosses to Pam and hands it to her.*)

LIZZIE. It's what you get for fooling with things like them tarot cards. You mustn't call up powers, Miss Pam. (*Pam is trying her best not to snap.*)

PAM. Please get the doctor's bag.

LIZZIE. I wish we were back in London.

PAM. (*Strong.*) Lizzie!

LIZZIE. I'm going, I'm going. (*Lizzie exits* R. *Max enters from outside, pushes aside the other French door so Roddy can enter easily with Stella in his arms. Pam stands.*)

MAX. Better put her down on the couch. (*Roddy crosses to sofa and puts Stella down.*)

PAM. What happened?

MAX. She ran straight for the edge.

PAM. Give her some of this. (*Pam hands her glass to Roddy. He makes Stella sip. She coughs, sits up.*)

STELLA. (*Timidly.*) I . . . I think you must hate me.

PAM. No, because we understand.

STELLA. Nobody could possibly understand.

RODDY. (*Stands.*) Dr. Scott should have a look at her.

MAX. I'll get him. (*He exits* R.)

STELLA. I saw her, Roddy.

RODDY. Saw who?

STELLA. Outside on the cliff . . . she was there . . . like a mist . . . like a cloud that was almost a woman . . . calling me to her.

PAM. (*A plea for help.*) Roddy, what are we going to do?

RODDY. (*Thoughtfully.*) I wish I knew. (*Note: Consult production notes on how to manage the following stage effects that happen almost simultaneously: A rush of wind is followed by lights going out, plunging the room into near total darkness. The glow in the fireplace casts bizarre shadows. The curtains or drapes at the French doors begin to blow and billow. That eerie melody returns.) Look! (He points L. Pam screams. In the dim light we can make out something standing at the open French doors, something not quite human, filmy, indistinct, cloudy. The twisted melody rises louder and louder.)*

STELLA. I must go to her! (*Stella tries to get up, but Roddy holds her back.*)

RODDY. No, Stella, no! (*The "apparition" raises its arms as if beckoning. French doors begin to bang menacingly.*)

PAM. Leave us alone! (*Desperate.*) Leave us alone, please! (*The unearthly melody reaches a terrifying crescendo. Stella and Roddy cling to one another. The French doors continue to bang open and shut until—*)

CURTAIN

ACT II

SCENE 2

AT RISE: *The following morning.*
Lizzie moves about the room tidying up. It's a warm day and sunlight streams in at the windows. This "calm" is in sharp contrast to the theatrics of the previous scene.

LIZZIE. (*Mumbles.*) Half a mind to pack up and leave . . . If I didn't care for them so much . . . and they didn't need me to look after them . . . I might just do it . . . tarot cards and carryings-on . . .

MRS. JESSUP. (*Offstage.*) 'Allo. (*Lizzie moves to the French doors.*)

LIZZIE. That you, Mrs. Jessup?

MRS. JESSUP. (*Offstage.*) It's me, Lizzie. (*Lizzie continues to tidy up. Mrs. Jessup enters.*) A lovely day, isn't it?

LIZZIE. Give me the day anytime. It's the nights I don't fancy. Especially in this place. (*Clearly, Mr. Jessup has gotten wind of "something" and is eager for more.*)

40

MRS. JESSUP. What went on last night? (*Lizzie is surprised, stops her tidying.*)

LIZZIE. Who told you?

MRS. JESSUP. Told me what?

LIZZIE. Now, now, dear, don't play games with Lizzie Flynn. You look like you're about to pounce on a quail. (*Lizzie continues with her work.*)

MRS. JESSUP. I heard it from the Commander's housekeeper.

LIZZIE. Heard what?

MRS. JESSUP. Dr. Scott called him up in the dead of night and said Miss Stella had a fainting spell and was spending the evening here.

LIZZIE. (*Stops her tidying.*) You haven't heard much, then. (*Mrs. Jessup, eager for more, sits* D. L. C., *leans forward.*)

MRS. JESSUP. What *did* happen? (*Lizzie pauses thoughtfully before answering.*)

LIZZIE. They were reading tarot cards.

MRS. JESSUP. That's all?

LIZZIE. I'll tell if you promise not to breathe a word.

MRS. JESSUP. I give you my solemn oath. (*Lizzie crosses to her, confidential tone.*)

LIZZIE. She tried to throw herself over the cliff.

MRS. JESSUP. (*Delighted with the news.*) No! (*Fakes horror.*) What a terrible thing. She must have been out of her head.

LIZZIE. Not only that, but something funny happened with Miss Carey.

MRS. JESSUP. Who's she?

LIZZIE. A houseguest. She's an actress.

MRS. JESSUP. Things happening to actresses—that's not unusual. You read about it all the time in the papers or see it on the telly.

LIZZIE. Be that as it may, she had a terrible fright.

MRS. JESSUP. The poor woman. Tsk, tsk.

LIZZIE. I don't know what happened exactly. They're cagey this morning. But from what I gather, they saw something they shouldn't have.

MRS. JESSUP. (*Fascinated.*) Same thing you saw on the stairway?

LIZZIE. Soon as I find out for myself, I'll tell you, Mrs. Jessup.

MRS. JESSUP. I'd appreciate that, Lizzie. I think it's important to know what's going on here. After all, I have the neighboring farm. I have to protect myself and my Charlie.

LIZZIE. I don't know what chance we stand against spirits.

MRS. JESSUP. I always say it's not the dead who'll do a person harm—it's the living. I won't take up any more of your time. I want to tell Charlie about Miss Stella. (*She stands, moves to French doors.*)

LIZZIE. 'Ere, now, Mrs. Jessup. I thought you weren't going to breathe a word.

MRS. JESSUP. Charlie? Charlie don't count. He's my husband. (*She exits.*)

LIZZIE. (*Mumbles to herself.*) I'd like to hear what Charlie says about that. (*Stella enters R. She wears same frock she wore in previous scene.*)

STELLA. Good morning, Lizzie.

LIZZIE. Are you feeling better, miss?

STELLA. Yes, yes, I am. Thank you. (*Stella is subdued. She crosses to the sofa, sits.*)

LIZZIE. Would you like some coffee?

STELLA. No. Please don't fuss. (*Pam enters right in time to overhear.*)

PAM. Lizzie, you might give some thought to lunch, although I doubt if anyone will be hungry. (*She crosses to D. R. C. chair.*)

LIZZIE. Will Miss Wendy be staying much longer?

PAM. I don't believe so.

LIZZIE. Good. If you ask me, she's to blame for what happened. (*Exits R.*) Tarot cards. Ha!

PAM. Did you sleep at all?

STELLA. I've never slept so soundly. I don't know what Dr. Scott gave me. I suppose Grandfather is furious.

PAM. (*Sits.*) I don't think he'll ever permit you to visit again. I'm sorry that the first night you slept here was so trying.

STELLA. I have a confession. It wasn't the first time.

PAM. I meant since you were a child.

STELLA. Do you remember the time you and Roddy went into Bristol? I called you that day. Grandfather was in the hospital.

PAM. I remember.

STELLA. I came to the house, let myself in. I was alone. Quite alone. Lizzie was gone, too. (*Pam is deeply concerned.*)

PAM. She spent the night with the Jessups. Stella, that was a *dangerous* thing to do.

STELLA. I knew she was here, my mother. I could smell her

perfume. She was in the nursery . . . weeping. (*Roddy enters* L. *Pam gestures him not to speak, to allow Stella to finish.*)

PAM. Weren't you afraid?

STELLA. Oh, no. My mother loves me. I know that now. I was happier than I have ever been in my life. I just lay, warm and quiet, watching the light, and knowing that she was near.

PAM. What light?

STELLA. The baby's night light. I thought, maybe, you or Lizzie went off and forgot about it. (*Sound of knocking at offstage door,* R.)

RODDY. I wouldn't dwell on it, Stella.

STELLA. (*Turns.*) How's Miss Carey?

RODDY. Out with Max, watching him sketch.

STELLA. It was dishonest of me, but when I knew you'd be gone, I had to come here. You understand, don't you? I had to. (*Lizzie enters.*)

LIZZIE. It's Commander Brooke. (*Commander Brooke strides into the room, once again ready for battle. Lizzie exits, Roddy crosses.*)

RODDY. (*Extends his hand.*) Good morning, Commander. (*Commander Brooke ignores Roddy's hand, moves* D. R. *of sofa.*)

COMMANDER BROOKE. If you had followed my wishes, Stella, and put this house out of your mind, none of this would have happened.

STELLA. I'm not harmed, Grandfather.

COMMANDER BROOKE. Rubbish. Dr. Scott told me about your dash from the house, your exhaustion. I understand some malignant presence was seen.

PAM. I'm afraid that's true. However, Stella thinks that the presence is a gentle and loving one.

RODDY. (*Moves* D. C.) You're familiar with the local interpretation of all this?

COMMANDER BROOKE. I am only *too* familiar with it.

RODDY. I think it's time you helped us with any information you may have.

COMMANDER BROOKE. I can give you no help whatever! I refuse, absolutely, to discuss my private memories with unscrupulous intruders— (*Calms down.*) I beg your pardon. I tell you, these phantasms are delusions, the hysterical delusions of ignorant minds. My daughter—my daughter is at rest. Are you

43

so superstitious as to credit village stories? So cynical as to imagine that a soul like my daughter, an unstained, saintly spirit, is doomed to walk the night, terrifying harmless people, including her own child?

STELLA. She loves me, Grandfather, I know she does. But my mother isn't happy. She can't rest. There's something that she wants, and there may be something that I could do.

COMMANDER BROOKE. Stella, you must stop this at once.

STELLA. I must find out. I must.

COMMANDER BROOKE. Mary is at rest, I tell you.

STELLA. But she isn't, Grandfather, I would face anything to give her rest.

COMMANDER BROOKE. Why do you torment me in this fashion? Why do you torment yourself? (*To Pam.*) Is Stella to go through life burdened with the thought that in this house is her mother's spirit—with that dreadful, blasphemous belief?

PAM. I have never heard a woman praised and remembered as your daughter is, Commander Brooke.

COMMANDER BROOKE. Yes—and her daughter is secretive, cunning, disobedient, a trickster—

STELLA. (*Excited, jumps up.*) No, Grandfather, that's not true. (*Embraces him.*) I'm none of those things! (*Stella dissolves into tears. Miss Holloway steps into the room, R.*)

MISS HOLLOWAY. (*Soothingly.*) There, there, Stella. You mustn't excite yourself. (*All look R. Miss Holloway is a tall woman dressed in a rather theatrical fashion. Her voice is strong, but gentle and smoothly modulated.*) Come here, my dear. (*Stella moves to Miss Holloway, who embraces her in a professional manner.*)

STELLA. Oh, Miss Holloway. It isn't true what Grandfather said.

PAM. (*Stands.*) Miss Holloway?

COMMANDER BROOKE. I called Miss Holloway as soon as I heard from Dr. Scott.

MISS HOLLOWAY. A long rest is what you need, Stella. You mustn't allow your emotions to rule you. Rest and positive thoughts are what you require. You're exhausted.

RODDY. You couldn't have come at a better time, Miss Holloway.

MISS HOLLOWAY. Indeed.

44

PAM. I hope you'll be able to spare us a few minutes. (*Miss Holloway thinks this over.*)

MISS HOLLOWAY. Stella, my car's outside. We'll join you shortly.

STELLA. Must I leave?

MISS HOLLOWAY. You must trust me, Stella. I have only your welfare at heart.

COMMANDER BROOKE. Do as she asked, Stella.

STELLA. Yes, Grandfather. (*Stella exits* R.)

PAM. (*Gestures* D. L. C.) Won't you sit down, Miss Holloway? (*Miss Holloway crosses, sits.*)

COMMANDER BROOKE. Stella is far from well. She is her father's daughter. When Mary died I retired from the navy and dedicated my life to one purpose—to make Mary's child the woman Mary would have wished her to be.

RODDY. Commander Brooke, Stella is not a child.

COMMANDER BROOKE. I believe I am the better judge of that. You force me to send Stella away . . . you force me to send her away from home. Now, if you'll excuse me. (*He exits* R. *No one speaks, until:*)

RODDY. Lord, I'm sorry for him! He's a sick man. If he sends her away, it will kill him. He'll never see her again.

MISS HOLLOWAY. I doubt that, Mr. Fitzgerald. (*Miss Holloway is, indeed, a remarkable woman and the actress playing the role must take the stage with considerable flair.*)

PAM. He's being torn to pieces. (*Pam is behind the sofa, Roddy* C. *Miss Holloway's manner is cool and assured.*)

MISS HOLLOWAY. You are in trouble. Can I help you some way?

PAM. (*Eases into it.*) You lived with Stella for some years, didn't you?

MISS HOLLOWAY. I sacrificed ten years of my career to complete the work Mary had begun. That was my tribute to my martyred friend. I have not regretted it.

PAM. We thought you would, perhaps, tell us whether Mary Meredith—whether she went through some great sorrow at Cliff End. We hear so much weeping.

MISS HOLLOWAY. Sorrow was Mary's portion, but she did not weep. Mary has passed to higher spheres.

45

RODDY. We have no right to ask, but we think that possibly her grief, her emotions, may have some influence in the house. If we could understand it—

PAM. You'd be doing us a great kindness.

MISS HOLLOWAY. I understand. I will try. (*As she speaks, Pam sits on sofa. Both she and Roddy hang on every word.*) I met Mary Me. edith at a nursing home. I was employed there. Mary had been sent to recuperate after influenza. My life's purpose found a deep response in her spirit.

RODDY. Life's purpose?

MISS HOLLOWAY. To create a center of healing which would use means beyond the physical. Mary had money inherited from her mother, and she was eager to use it in doing good. However, there followed the journey to Spain, that disastrous marriage and the entrance of that evil genius into Mary's beautiful life.

PAM. Carmel. (*Miss Holloway nods. Roddy sits on the end of the sofa.*)

MISS HOLLOWAY. They were all together here at Cliff End when I was sent for. Mary required a private nurse. It was apparent to me that her illness was due to grief and shock.

RODDY. Due to what?

MISS HOLLOWAY. I should think that was fairly obvious. *Carmel's infatuation* and Llewellyn's dubious charm.

PAM. You mean she had fallen in love with Llewellyn Meredith?

MISS HOLLOWAY. Love? I'd hardly call it that. Neither of those two were capable of love.

PAM. Mary permitted Carmel to remain?

MISS HOLLOWAY. You don't help the weak to overcome their sin by removing them from temptation. With anyone less depraved than those two, Mary's tender guidance would have prevailed. Mary even trusted Carmel with her baby. Mary's own charity deceived her, but not for long. She had sacrificed herself for Carmel, but she would not sacrifice her child. She sent for me.

PAM. Was Carmel harming Stella?

MISS HOLLOWAY. The baby did nothing but cry. Carmel would rush to her, cover her with kisses. She was destroying the child. Broke all discipline, ignored all rules. I forbade her to enter the nursery.

PAM. What of Meredith?

MISS HOLLOWAY. He travelled much of the time, amusing

46

himself. Eventually he secured employment for Carmel in Paris in a fashion house.

PAM. Free from Carmel, I expect you had peace—you, Mary and Stella.

MISS HOLLOWAY. For two perfect years. Mary created an atmosphere of heavenly serenity. We studied together. Commander Brooke came sometimes, but only when Llewellyn was away. Then—Carmel returned. In spite of the most solemn promises to remain abroad, she returned. Meredith was here at the time. I shall never forget the look on his face. Carmel, once a beauty, was a bedraggled, hollow-cheeked creature. Life had not treated her kindly. He stared at her and went up to his studio for Mary and locked himself in. I hoped Mary would order Carmel from the house. She didn't.

RODDY. Why didn't Meredith throw her out?

MISS HOLLOWAY. He proposed to paint her.

PAM. Good lord!

MISS HOLLOWAY. (Stands.) I heard him talking about it to Mary. He said he had a first-class idea.

RODDY. I think we know what that "first-class" idea was. To paint her as she was and, then, show what she had become.

MISS HOLLOWAY. Yes.

PAM. Did Carmel suspect what he was doing?

MISS HOLLOWAY. No. She was madly "in love" with him still. I blame Llewellyn for what happened. (As she speaks, she stands, looks to the portrait of Mary.) It was he who drove Carmel into a frenzy. A storm had been raging all day and the wind at Cliff End always made him insufferable. He had finished the portrait. "Come and look at it," Mary called to Carmel. Llewellyn was laughing. Next thing I heard was Carmel's scream. She was hysterical. He told her she could get out now, his work was finished. There was no place for her. She ran to the nursery, snatched up little Stella. Mary followed, hoping to calm her. I got the infant from Carmel. In her state, I fully believe she meant to take her revenge out on Stella. (Her recitation becomes more and more vivid.) She cursed out at Mary. Then she ran in here and out through the doors, to the cliff. Mary followed. Carmel had been shamming, I suppose. I saw her make a clutch at the tree and check herself at the edge. Mary flung herself toward Carmel to pull her back and then— (Dramatic pause.)

47

PAM. Please go on.

MISS HOLLOWAY. I will say to you what I have never said before to anyone. (*Another pause.*) As Mary swayed there, on the edge of death, *I saw Carmel's arm swing out and strike her on the head.*) Mary went over without a cry. (*Pause.*) Carmel died a few days later, in my arms. I nursed her day and night, but she was almost gone when they brought her to me. (*Checks her watch.*) Now I must say goodbye.

PAM. Thank you, Miss Holloway. (*Miss Holloway moves* R.)

RODDY. One question. (*Miss Holloway stops.*)

MISS HOLLOWAY. Yes?

RODDY. Was it against your rules to have a light in the nursery?

MISS HOLLOWAY. Certainly.

RODDY. Did Mrs. Meredith agree?

MISS HOLLOWAY. Our minds were as one. I trust I have made you both realize that if some troublesome spirit haunts Cliff End, it is not Mary's. I'll show myself out. (*She exits. Roddy moves to entry, watching her depart, offstage.*)

RODDY. I have the feeling we ought to applaud. What do you make of all that?

PAM. What she meant us to make of it. It's Carmel who weeps. (*Roddy moves* L. *of sofa.*)

RODDY. What a household! Meredith a cynic, Carmel a vixen, Holloway a wire-pulling hypocrite, and Mary a—

PAM. Prig?

RODDY. Well, say a creature "too good for human nature." Of course, it may be Holloway who's the prig. We are seeing Mary through her eyes.

PAM. It can't go on, Roddy. Someone will be hurt.

RODDY. We could shut up the nursery.

PAM. That won't be enough.

RODDY. Either we make peace with whatever haunts Cliff End, or it drives us from the house. If that happens, we lose everything. Flat broke with nothing to show for it. (*Looks to portrait.*) If only the Commander's daughter could speak.

PAM. I'm out of love with Mary Meredith. Think of leaving the baby in Holloway's cold hands. Holloway certainly hates Carmel. She probably strangled her.

RODDY. In pneumonia, a little neglect goes quite a long way. (*Pam reacts to the suggestion.*)

48

PAM. We've been making ourselves polite to a murderess?
RODDY. I'm ready to believe it. I wouldn't mind trying to prove it, if only we could call a ghost into court.
PAM. Perhaps we can.
RODDY. I'm not following.
PAM. If a spirit is trying to communicate with us, there is one thing that we ought to try. We could hold a seance.
RODDY. A seance?
PAM. Yes.
RODDY. When?
PAM. Tonight.

FAST CURTAIN

END OF ACT II

ACT III

AT RISE: *That evening. Prior to curtain, sound of howling wind.*

Wendy sits on the sofa, wiping the table with a dust cloth. There's a candle on the table. Max stands at the fireplace, fire glowing, inking in letters on a deck of cards, one letter to each card. The drapes are open.

MAX. I hope I'm doing this right. I put one letter of the alphabet on each card. "A" on one, "B" on another, et cetera.
WENDY. With two additional cards. One for "Yes," one for "No."
MAX. Sure you're up to this? You gave us a shock last evening. (*Wendy stops, reflects.*)
WENDY. I was perfectly all right with you on the beach today.
MAX. Quite recovered.
WENDY. I realize now I didn't see myself in the mirror. (*Max stops, amazed.*) It was Carmel. The other Carmel—the one Meredith painted when her beauty was gone. (*Max has finished with the marking, crosses to Wendy, hands cards to her.*)
MAX. Chap was something of a sadist. Still, we must remember the artist has certain prerogatives.
WENDY. Spoken like a true chauvinist. (*She begins to set the cards out in a circle atop the table.*)
MAX. I resent that.
WENDY. I know you well enough, Max. You're a sensitive man. You respect feelings. You'd never paint so viciously.
MAX. I don't believe I'd show the finished product to the model.
WENDY. You might—if you wanted to hurt the model. Undoubtedly, that's what Meredith planned for. (*Wendy continues to lay out the cards. Lizzie enters R. with a wine glass.*)
LIZZIE. Will this do? (*Moves behind sofa, hands wine glass to Wendy.*)
WENDY. The glass has to be thin.
LIZZIE. There's none thinner in the house.
MAX. Let me have a look. (*Wendy hands him the wine glass.*

He holds it up to his ear, clinks against it with his finger, listens.)
It's got vibration. *(Hands it back to Wendy.)*
WENDY. We're almost ready.
LIZZIE. *(Looks at cards.)* What sort of heathen mischief are you up to now?
WENDY. We're hoping to make contact. *(Lizzie looks grim.)*
LIZZIE. With whom, may I ask?
MAX. Mary Meredith, we think.
LIZZIE. *(Dubious.)* She's going to come out from wherever she is and talk to you, is that it?
WENDY. It doesn't happen that way.
LIZZIE. I wouldn't know.
WENDY. The spirit will spell out things with the glass.
LIZZIE. What if the spirit don't know how to spell? *(Knock at the front door. Lizzie is cynical about Wendy's efforts.)* Maybe that's Mary Meredith. *(She exits R.)*
WENDY. Negativism won't help. I know what makes that awful cold.
MAX. *(Moves D. L. C., sits.)* Incidentally, Roddy and Pam had something of a go. Seems Roddy has experienced that chill and depression, but didn't say so because he was afraid Pam would make too much of it.
WENDY. No sense in Roddy denying anything at this point. If a spirit is to materialize, it has to draw something from the human bodies within reach. It drains warmth and strength. *(Finished with the cards.)* There. We're ready, I think. *(Dr. Scott enters R.)*
DR. SCOTT. Ah, Miss Carey.
WENDY. I didn't know you were stopping by.
DR. SCOTT. Had to check on a farmhand. Nail went through his foot. Since I was close, I thought I might see how you were doing.
WENDY. I do appreciate your concern, but I'm quite recovered, anxious to get on with it.
DR. SCOTT. On with it?
MAX. Wendy is conducting a seance.
DR. SCOTT. Do you think that's wise, Miss Carey?
WENDY. It can't do any harm.
DR. SCOTT. I'm not so confident.
MAX. You disapprove?
DR. SCOTT. You were in a state last evening. Highly emotional.

51

WENDY. So was everyone else, including yourself, Doctor, if I can be permitted an observation.

DR. SCOTT. True, true. (*Pam enters* R.)

PAM. Nice to see you again, Doctor. (*Dr. Scott has his eye on the table.*)

DR. SCOTT. Checking on my patient. She looks fit. Is that how you do it? The seance. With cards and a glass?

WENDY. One way.

DR. SCOTT. You know, I've never been to a seance. I've always been intrigued. (*It's obvious he wants to be asked. Roddy enters from nursery.*)

RODDY. Getting close to zero hour?

WENDY. Don't joke.

RODDY. I didn't mean to. There's nothing unusual in the nursery. No music box and I've disconnected the lamps.

WENDY. What about the wind chime?

RODDY. I took it down.

PAM. Dr. Scott would like to join us.

DR. SCOTT. If it wouldn't be an imposition.

RODDY. (*Crosses* D. C.) I think it would be an excellent idea if you remained. You're familiar with the house and you knew the Merediths.

WENDY. Please do, Dr. Scott.

DR. SCOTT. Delighted.

PAM. Why was the nursery so far from the other rooms?

DR. SCOTT. Miss Holloway insisted. She had strong beliefs on child-rearing.

WENDY. (*Tentative.*) We can begin. (*They look to one another, not certain what's expected of them.*) Dr. Scott, if you'll get a chair. (*Dr. Scott takes the chair from* D. R. *and places it* R. *of table, sits.*) Pam and Roddy with me. Max, you here. (*She indicates the* D. R. C. *chair. Max moves it close to the table, sits. Roddy and Pam sit on the sofa, Pam to the* R. *of Wendy, Roddy to the* L. *While they seat themselves, Lizzie returns* R.)

LIZZIE. If I had known what you were up to, I would have made plans to spend the night with the Jessups. I'm going to lock myself in my room, and I won't come out, no matter what I hear.

PAM. You could join us.

RODDY. After all, you saw the ghost.

LIZZIE. Join you! I'd sooner lost my teeth. You may be keen as mustard for this seance, but don't try to drag in Lizzie Flynn.

PAM. We understand your position.

WENDY. Would you close the drapes, Lizzie, and turn down the lights? (*Lizzie wavers at this request.*)

LIZZIE. It's against my better judgment, but I'll do it. (*She crosses to drapes and draws them shut.*)

WENDY. I'll act as medium, the channel of communication between the earthly world and the spirit world. It's important that we each concentrate as hard as possible. Whatever you do, don't allow any doubts to cloud your concentration. (*She takes a match and lights the candle.*) I'll turn the glass over and, then, we'll each put one finger lightly to the bottom. (*She turns over the glass. Lizzie crosses R. Fingers are placed to the glass.*)

DR. SCOTT. Like this?

WENDY. Yes. (*Pause.*) The lights, Lizzie. (*Lizzie shakes her head disapprovingly, puts her hand to some switch, exits R. The room is now illuminated by the glow from the fireplace and the flickering candle on the table. A sense of nervous excitement is in the atmosphere.*)

RODDY. How do we begin?

WENDY. First we must clear our minds of anything except this house and what's happened here. We can take turns asking questions but no one must overreact if anything should disturb the seance. Agreed?

OTHERS. Agreed. (*The seance is conducted soberly, with an almost-measured beat, nothing rushed.*)

WENDY. I'll begin. (*Long pause.*) Is there someone who wants to communicate with us? (*Nothing.*) We want to help you. (*Rush of wind.*) Are you there, Mary Meredith? (*Again, nothing.*) Is there someone there? (*Pause.*) Please. (*Nothing.*) We're waiting. (*The glass slowly moves to a card.*)

PAM. The glass—

DR. SCOTT. It's moving.

WENDY. Keep your fingers on it.

RODDY. It's going to the card marked . . . "YES."

WENDY. What is your name? (*Note: After each question, the glass will move to some card indicating or spelling out the response.*)

MAX. (*Watching the traveling glass.*) It's moved to the letter "M."

RODDY. Are you Mary Meredith? (*Glass moves. The glow appears on the portrait.*)

DR. SCOTT. "YES."

PAM. Did you die at Cliff End? (*Glass moves.*) "YES."

MAX. Did you die a natural death? (*Glass moves.*) "NO."

RODDY. A violent death? (*Glass moves.*) "YES."

PAM. Was it an accident? (*Glass moves.*) "NO."

DR. SCOTT. Do you blame someone for your death? (*Glass moves.*) "YES."

PAM. Did Carmel strike you? (*Glass moves.*) "YES."

RODDY. Do you know that Carmel is dead? (*Glass moves.*) "YES."

MAX. Do you want Carmel punished? (*Glass moves.*) "YES."

WENDY. Do you have a purpose in remaining? (*Glass moves.*) "YES."

PAM. Can you tell us what it is? (*Glass spells out the answer, moving from card to card.*)

MAX. (*Spelling along as the glass moves.*) I-G-U-A-R-D. I guard.

DR. SCOTT. You mean you guard this house against some danger? (*Glass moves.*) "YES."

WENDY. From where does this danger come? (*Glass moves.*) "C."

MAX. From Carmel? (*Glass moves.*) "YES."

DR. SCOTT. Whom is Carmel trying to injure? (*Glass spells out name.*)

RODDY. S-T-E-L-L-A. Stella.

PAM. Mary was with Stella in the nursery. Don't you see, that may be what Mary wants—the thing that has kept her haunting and restless—longing for her child and it's the child that Carmel wants to harm.

RODDY. Stella said she was warm and safe in the nursery. Yet the night she ran for the cliff, she experienced that terrible cold.

PAM. Precisely. The terrible cold of Carmel's evil.

MAX. There are *two* ghosts to deal with, not one.

DR. SCOTT. It's a deadlock, I'm afraid. (*Suddenly, the glass skids across the table.*)

PAM. The glass! It's moving too fast!

WENDY. Don't let go of it!

MAX. It's spelling something out. (*Glass slows for the spelling.*)
L-I-E-S. Lies.

PAM. I don't understand.

WENDY. Ask something else. Quickly.

PAM. What should we do? (*Glass spells out answer.*) S-E-N-D-
H-E-R-A-W-A-Y. You mean we should send Stella away? (*Glass
moves again, spelling out answer.*) N-O. C-A-R-M-E-L.

RODDY. She wants us to get rid of Carmel.

DR. SCOTT. What can we do to make her go? Exorcism? (*Glass
moves.*) "NO."

WENDY. Mary Meredith, try to tell us what we should do.
(*Glass moves.*) G-O. Go.

RODDY. Why must we go? (*Glass spells out answer.*) D-A-N-
G-E-R. What is the danger? Tell us. (*Nothing.*) Tell us! (*The
glass goes wild. They can't hold it. It skids to the floor. Glow
fades on the portrait.*)

MAX. The glass—

DR. SCOTT. I couldn't hold on. (*Wendy shuts her eyes, moans.*)

RODDY. Wendy, what is it?

WENDY. (*Trancelike, she mutters the words, her voice unlike
her own.*) Nina mia, nina mia—

MAX. (*Jumps to his feet.*) Wendy!

DR. SCOTT. (*Cautiously.*) Don't disturb her.

PAM. She's speaking Spanish.

WENDY. *Nina mia, chica, guapa . . . Stella, nina mia . . .*

DR. SCOTT. (*Translating.*) My darling . . . my baby . . . my
darling little girl . . .

WENDY. *Stella, nina mia . . . chica . . .* (*A glow appears on
the wooden chest by the nursery door—consult production notes—
howl of wind. Wendy, trancelike.*) *Nina mia . . . chica Stella . . .*

MAX. Why would Mary Meredith speak in Spanish?

RODDY. (*Logically.*) Because it isn't Mary Meredith. It's Carmel
speaking.

DR. SCOTT. (*Notices glow on chest.*) Look. (*All look L. Slowly,
Wendy "comes out of it."*)

MAX. Roddy, what's in that chest? (*Roddy gets up, moves to
chest. Dr. Scott and Max are with him.*)

PAM. Are you all right? (*Wendy nods her head "yes."*)

MAX. (*Sniffs.*) What's that strong perfume? It's coming from the
chest.

RODDY. (*Recognizes it.*) *Mimosa*. (*He drops to one knee, opens chest.*)

PAM. But *mimosa* was Mary's scent. (*Roddy takes the perfume flask from the chest, pulls stopper, sniffs.*)

RODDY. There was no scent when we first found this bottle. There is now.

DR. SCOTT. (*Points into chest.*) These were Carmel's things.

WENDY. She's directed you to the chest. She wanted you to open it. She wanted you to find the perfume.

PAM. But the initial on the bottle is "G."

RODDY. (*Rubs hard.*) The bottle's old and it's encrusted with dirt. (*Harder.*) If I clean it a bit, I . . . think . . . we'll . . . discover . . . the "G" . . . is, actually, "C."

MAX. Carmel.

PAM. But Stella says *mimosa* was her mother's favorite scent. Carmel could have stolen the bottle from Mary.

DR. SCOTT. In that case, the bottle would have "M" on it, not "C."

WENDY. Maybe it was Carmel spelling out "lies, lies." (*She gets glass, puts it back on the table.*) Help me, Pam. (*They repeat business with glass. Others watch.*) Carmel, are you in this room? Are you with us now? (*The glass moves.*)

PAM. "YES."

WENDY. Is this what you are trying to tell us—that you are Stella's mother? (*Nothing.*) It's not moving.

MAX. Try again.

WENDY. Carmel, are you Stella's mother? (*Sound of doors rattling behind drapes.*)

MAX. The wind's at the doors. (*He crosses to drapes, opens them, secures doors. Dialogue through this business.*)

PAM. There. The glass is moving again.

WENDY. Carmel, are you Stella's mother? (*Glass moves.*)

PAM. "YES." (*Sound of door open and shutting offstage R. All look, not knowing who or what is about to enter. It's Stella. Glow on chest out.*)

RODDY. Stella! (*He crosses to her, switches on lights.*) We thought you were with Miss Holloway.

STELLA. I couldn't stay. I had to come back. When no one was looking, I simply walked out. I took a cab from the station.

56

PAM. She can't remain here. Roddy, it's too risky. (*Stella crosses to* D. C.)

STELLA. It's as if something were pulling me to Cliff End; I couldn't resist.

RODDY. Stella, who told you *mimosa* was your mother's perfume?

STELLA. (*Thinks.*) I don't remember, but I've always known it was true. Is it important?

MAX. Roddy, the ghost could be tricking us.

RODDY. I don't think so. In the nursery, Stella felt love and warmth. It was her mother's spirit that lighted the baby lamp.

STELLA. What's been happening?

RODDY. Sit down, Stella. (*She does,* D. L. C., *aware that something unusual and climactic in her life is about to happen. Roddy steps toward her.*)

PAM. It was your mother who was with you in the nursery.

STELLA. I know that, yes. I told you.

PAM. It was your mother who made you happy, but, Stella, it was not Mary Meredith. That was a lie. You are not Mary Meredith's child. (*All look at Stella, wondering how she will take the news. She speaks in a low voice.*)

STELLA. I did wonder sometimes . . . I'm so unlike her. Grandfather reminded me enough . . . and Miss Holloway.

PAM. (*Comfortingly.*) You can be yourself now, not an imitation Mary.

STELLA. Do you know who my mother was? Can it have been Carmel?

PAM. Yes, we're sure of it. (*Max gets the book containing "The Artist's Model." He hands it to Stella, opened to the page.*)

STELLA. (*Looks at page.*) I have seen her face in my father's sketches and I always loved it. They say she was wicked, but of course it's not true. Her face is as loving and kind as the voice in the nursery. Think of Grandfather, cheated all these years. I'm the child of that girl he despised and that man he detested, and he has given me everything.

DR. SCOTT. He's had a loving companion who was attentive and loyal to him.

WENDY. That's more than a daughter of Mary Meredith would have been. (*From the nursery comes the sound of weeping.*)

DR. SCOTT. Listen. (*All tense, listen.*)

PAM. The weeping again. (*A pause and then the sound of the music box—melancholy and forlorn.*)

MAX. Don't tell me that's a wind chime.

RODDY. It means Carmel is there.

STELLA. In the nursery now?

RODDY. Yes.

STELLA. I must go to her.

PAM. Roddy, be careful.

RODDY. How do you feel about it, Stella?

STELLA. I think I will be happier all my life if I go into the nursery now, alone—

DR. SCOTT. I don't think that's advisable, Stella.

STELLA. *Alone.* (*Stella has spoken the single word with such conviction and determination that the others in the room are taken aback. Stella appears quite adult and rational.*)

DR. SCOTT. (*Resigned.*) Very well. (*Stella stands, turns to face the nursery door, crosses over, the book in her hand.*)

RODDY. Stella— (*Stella turns.*) We're here, just outside the door.

STELLA. (*Smiles warmly.*) You needn't worry. (*She pauses before entering, goes into the nursery and quietly closes the door. Music box out.*)

DR. SCOTT. If anything happens to Stella, I shall blame myself. (*Sound of thunder.*)

RODDY. We had no choice, Dr. Scott. Otherwise, Stella would spend the rest of her life in doubt, under the not-so-tender care of Nurse Holloway.

MAX. (*Steps to the French doors, looks out.*) We're in for a storm.

WENDY. Mary Meredith certainly fooled Biddlecombe.

RODDY. Yes, everyone had a good word for her. Why not? She was native soil and Carmel was foreign dirt.

PAM. Neither Mary nor Holloway would permit a baby light in the nursery, but Carmel would.

WENDY. Mary Meredith would have made a fine actress.

MAX. She knew how to manipulate people.

PAM. (*To Wendy.*) I should have remembered something Miss Holloway said. It was *Mary* who called Carmel to the studio to look at the portrait. She obviously enjoyed playing with people's lives. Even to taking the baby from Carmel.

WENDY. But why would she do that?

RODDY. She did it to keep Meredith.

PAM. (*Points to cards.*) That's why she wanted us to send the spirit of Carmel from the house. Mary haunts only because of Carmel—for fear of Carmel telling the truth. (*Door to nursery opens. Dramatic pause. Stella steps out, a sweet smile on her face.*)

STELLA. She's gone . . . I could feel her presence . . . smell the *mimosa* . . . I called her *madre* and I heard her soft loving voice speak my name . . . then there was nothing but the sound of the wind . . . the *mimosa*, too, faded away. She's gone—in peace. (*Roddy crosses over, embraces her.*)

WENDY. Now Mary has no reason to haunt. Carmel is gone. Mary will follow. Oh! Brrrr. I'm so terribly cold.

PAM. (*Rubs her arms.*) So am I. It's worse than before. I can feel my blood turning to ice water. (*Thunder. The glow on Mary's portrait appears, the eerie melody returns. The French doors fling open as if enraged. The lights blackout—only the fireplace and the candle illuminate the room.*)

MAX. We're in for it now. The storm's going to be fierce.

RODDY. Don't be a fool! That's not a natural storm. It's Mary Meredith.

MAX. (*Frightened.*) What does she want?

RODDY. She's got nothing to lose now. She wants *revenge*. Max, quick, take Stella out of here. All of you, get out of this room.

PAM. What are you going to do?!

RODDY. *Get out of this room, I said!* (*Max grabs Stella. All exit R., leaving Roddy alone. Note: At this point all the effects come into full sway. The glow remains on the portrait, the wind and the eerie melody escalate. Going on sheer pluck, Roddy crosses to candle, picks it up. He moves to the portrait, speaking as he crosses U.*) Mary Meredith, you were a cold, hard, self-righteous prig! An overweening, hypocritical egoist. (*As if in reply, the French doors bang open and shut and open again. There, in the dimness, outside the house, is the spirit materialization of Mary Meredith—filmy, luminous, misty. Roddy sees it, gasps. The spirit raises its arms as if to strike Roddy down. Roddy swallows hard, moves to the manifestation, doing his best not to pass out.*) You pitiful trickster, you're finished! You're shown up! Your poses are done with, you shallow fraud! (*Roddy laughs nervously and the "form" agitates.*) You don't like laughter, do you? Well, you're something to laugh at, Mary Meredith. You're finished here unless you want to remain and hear people laughing at you. You couldn't stand that, could you? There is nothing left of you, Mary, but a story to laugh over—go and scare crows! (*The sound effects reach a crescendo. Roddy throws the candle—consult production notes—and the spirit of Mary Meredith goes from sight. The French doors slam shut with a bang. The general stage lighting returns, the glow on the portrait fades. Roddy stands L., breathing heavily. He makes his way to D. L. C., sits. Pam and Dr. Scott enter R., wary. Roddy anticipates their question.*) She's gone. She couldn't stand the sound of anyone laughing at her. Her time was up and she knew it. (*Dr. Scott moves to Roddy.*)

DR. SCOTT. You're all right?

RODDY. My heart's beating like a racehorse and I'm planning to pass out any minute, so stay close.

PAM. You don't think she'll return?

RODDY. Not a chance.

LIZZIE. (*Offstage.*) Miss Pamela! Mr. Roddy! (*Lizzie hurries in from R.*)

PAM. What is it, Lizzie? (*Lizzie moves into the room.*)

LIZZIE. It's Whiskey! He's come back. Jumped in the window, glad to be home, frisky as before, meowing for his dinner. What does it mean?

RODDY. It means, Lizzie, we are staying at Cliff End, the ghosts are gone, and I plan to see a great deal of Stella Meredith.

LIZZIE. (*Overjoyed.*) Lord bless us all!

PAM. Roddy, I have a wonderful idea!

RODDY. What?

PAM. You could write a play about all this! (*Roddy sighs, moves his wrist to Dr. Scott who immediately begins to take his pulse. Curtain.*)

THE END

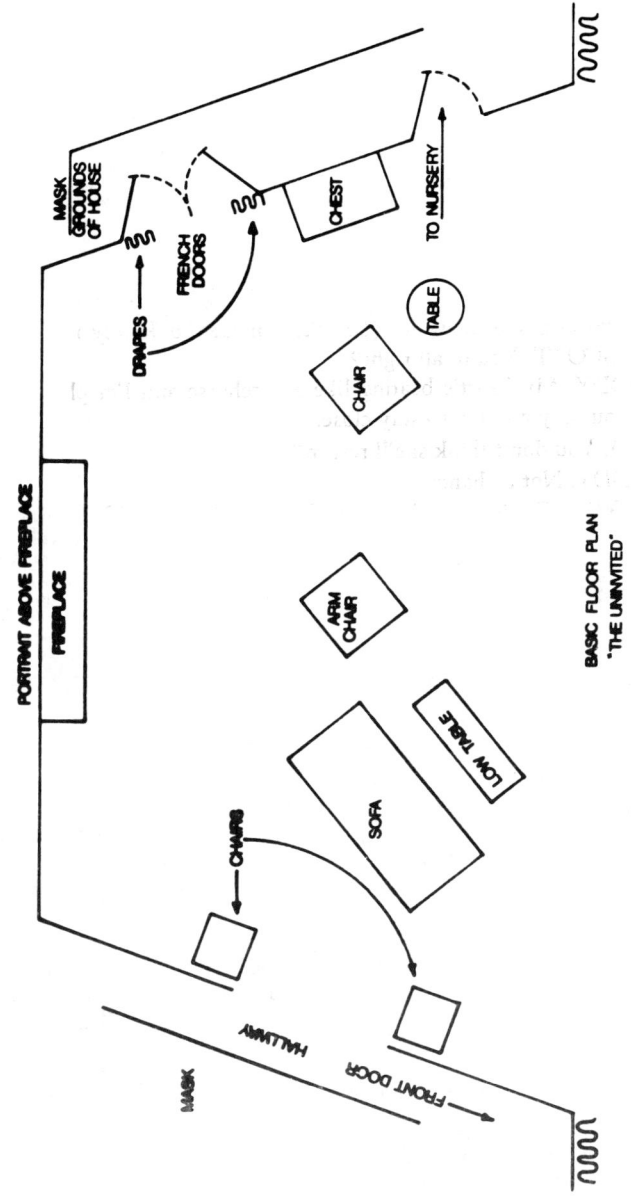

BASIC FLOOR PLAN
"THE UNINVITED"

PROPERTIES

ACT I, SCENE 1: *Onstage:* Chairs (2)—one on each side of entryway, fireplace with painting of Mary Meredith on wall above (U. C.), curtains or drapes at French doors (L.), sofa, low table (D. R.), armchair (D. R. C.), another chair with small side table (D. L. C.), white sheets over furniture, plus optional dressing, as desired: pictures, lamps, bric-a-brac, rugs, etc. *Brought on:* Walking stick (Commander Brooke), notebook and pencil (Roddy), handkerchief (Stella).

ACT I, SCENE 2: *Brought on:* Swatches of fabric (Pam), manuscript (Roddy), small trunk or chest containing rolled canvas, shawl, fan, perfume bottle with stopper (Roddy), covered basket (Mrs. Jessup), traveling coat (Pam).

ACT II, SCENE 1: *Onstage, added:* Radio, wine glasses, decanter, tarot cards with box, chest with shawl covering, flowers in vases. *Brought on:* Pencil (Max, at curtain), plate of appetizers (Lizzie), art book (Lizzie), cosmetic compact (Wendy, at curtain), watch (Miss Holloway).

ACT III: *Onstage, added:* Candle and matches, dust cloth (Wendy), cards and pen (Max, at curtain). *Brought on:* Wine glasses (Lizzie).

COSTUMES

The costuming is contemporary. Listed here are only those outfits that, in some way, are essential to the plot: Lizzie wears an apron (Act I Scene 2); smock (Pam; Act I Scene 2); jacket (Roddy; Act I Scene 2); funny hat (Mrs. Jessup; Act I Scene 2); dark dress with starched white apron (Lizzie; Act II Scene 1); dress or suit with a theatrical flair (Miss Holloway; Act II Scene 2).

NOTE: A nice costume touch can be achieved at the opening of Act II—the housewarming. Have actresses wear floor-length gowns and the men wear something a bit formal. This, of course, is optional, but it does make for a good "stage picture."

SOUND EFFECTS

Wind, thunder, door closing from offstage R. (manually), eerie melody when Mary's "presence" is in the room, birds, radio music, music box,

Carmel weeping (this can be easily handled by having actress or female member of crew stand behind the nursery door and "cry").

PRODUCTION NOTES
ON HOW TO MANAGE SPECIAL EFFECTS

There are innumerable ways to create the few effects mentioned in the text, depending on the resources and finances of the individual theatre group. This might involve everything from a fog machine for the ghostly appearances to a "luminous mist" appearing at the portrait (a hose attached to a sealed bag of hot ice backstage). If any of the more elaborate devices can be obtained *and work*, then use them by all means. However, the techniques listed here have all been thoroughly tested in performance. They work, they're inexpensive, they're simple to manage.

THE COLD:

There is no technical effect for this. Performers must act and react visibly to the "sensation" of cold in the room.

PORTRAIT OF MARY MEREDITH GLOWS:

The simplest way is to have a special light below or behind the portrait and "dim it up" when the text requires. If a follow spot is available, it can be thrown on the portrait from the front of the house, beginning with a "pin spot" and then widening out until the entire portrait is covered. The procedure is reversed when portrait "glow" fades back to normal.

BLUISH LIGHT FROM INTERIOR OF NURSERY:

The "blue light" represents the baby lamp. A special spot, offstage D. L., with blue gel, will give the desired effect, or a crew member can stand offstage holding an electrical or kerosene lamp. A blue bulb will work for the electrical lamp, and a blue gel held in front of the kerosene lamp will produce the same result.

LIGHTS GOING OUT:

A standard "blackout," except that the glow from the fireplace will remain (Act III).

THE SEANCE:

Again, this is something that is created largely by the acting and the room "atmosphere," e.g.—candlelight, fire in the hearth, closed drapes.

Performers should not rush the seance since the audience will be "spelling along" and part of the tension will be in discovering things at the same time the onstage characters do.

GLOW ON WOODEN CHEST:

Virtually the same requirements as glow on the portrait of Mary Meredith. Or a special light can be set up behind the chest. Even a flashlight will do. Simply have a small slit at the base of the scenery flat. A crew member can slip a hand through, holding the flashlight, snapping it on and off when required. A "fading up" effect can be worked with the flashlight by pressing it against the chest and, then, slowly pulling back so the illumination will spread. To "fade down," simply press the light close to the chest and snap it off. Pressing in close decreases the "light spill," creating the "fading" effect.

TOSSING LIGHTED CANDLE AT GHOST:

Just before Roddy tosses the candle at ghost, have fire in hearth blackout. At that moment have Roddy snuff out the candle with his thumb, the hand not holding the candle, or his breath. Immediately after this the candle is thrown. It should all happen "at once": Roddy yells—"There is nothing left of you, Mary, but a story to laugh over—go and scare crows!" Blackout as candle is snuffed and tossed (also check the ghost of Mary Meredith).

FRENCH DOORS OPEN AND BANG SHUT AND OPEN:

Have poles or rods at the outside bases of the doors and have stagehands, unseen, simply push back and forth from offstage.

WIND BLOWS DRAPES OR CURTAINS:

Electric fan(s) positioned above doors offstage L. will do the trick, but the fan should be of the silent-motor type. Another alternative is to use the large standing exhaust type of fan.

WINE GLASS SKIDDING ACROSS TABLE TO FLOOR:

Glass is manipulated wholly by the actors. When it "moves," it's because they are "pushing" it with their fingertips although the dialogue gives the impression the glass is moving of its own accord. Same is true when the glass skids to the floor. Actors give it a hard shove—as if some force were pulling it from the table.

THE GHOST OF MARY MEREDITH:

The "ghost" appears twice—*never clearly seen.* Each time outside the French doors. Once at the conclusion of Act II Scene 1, once at the near-end of the play. It is luminous, ethereal. A special "ghost light" can be rigged outside the doors for use only when the ghost appears. In Act III to make the ghost "disappear" from view, the ghost light blackouts at the same time the fireplace blackouts and the candle is tossed. Mary's ghost can be nothing more than a gown of chiffon or some filmy material, the face nothing more than a transparent mask obtained at any joke or costume shop. Long false hair adds to the desired effect. If there is fly space, the "ghost" can be let down via wire and pulled up the same way. If this presents any problems, then use an *additional performer* to play the role of Mary's ghost. The advantage here is that the actress is able to move quickly on her own and avoids the possibility of any technical foul-ups. A flashlight can be substituted for a ghost spot. Actress holds flashlight at waist level, the light beaming up on her face. It's snapped off when ghost disappears.

ACCEPTANCE OF THE FACT THERE ARE GHOSTS:

The characters in the play accept the phenomenon of spirits and never question it. Since they believe, the audience will have little difficulty in accepting the basic premise.

SPECIAL NOTE

It's a good idea to have a *minimum* of at least two technical rehearsals for the stage crew. Give the cast a couple of nights off to polish lines, and concentrate on getting the effects right and smoothing out any rough spots.

NEW PLAYS

★ GUARDIANS by Peter Morris. In this unflinching look at war, a disgraced American soldier discloses the truth about Abu Ghraib prison, and a clever English journalist reveals how he faked a similar story for the London tabloids. "Compelling, sympathetic and powerful." —NY Times. "Sends you into a state of moral turbulence." —Sunday Times (UK). "Nothing short of remarkable." —Village Voice. [1M, 1W] ISBN: 978-0-8222-2177-7

★ BLUE DOOR by Tanya Barfield. Three generations of men (all played by one actor), from slavery through Black Power, challenge Lewis, a tenured professor of mathematics, to embark on a journey combining past and present. "A teasing flare for words." —Village Voice. "Unfailingly thought-provoking." —LA Times. "The play moves with the speed and logic of a dream." —Seattle Weekly. [2M] ISBN: 978-0-8222-2209-5

★ THE INTELLIGENT DESIGN OF JENNY CHOW by Rolin Jones. This irreverent "techno-comedy" chronicles one brilliant woman's quest to determine her heritage and face her fears with the help of her astounding creation called Jenny Chow. "Boldly imagined." —NY Times. "Fantastical and funny." —Variety. "Harvests many laughs and finally a few tears." —LA Times. [3M, 3W] ISBN: 978-0-8222-2071-8

★ SOUVENIR by Stephen Temperley. Florence Foster Jenkins, a wealthy society eccentric, suffers under the delusion that she is a great coloratura soprano—when in fact the opposite is true. "Hilarious and deeply touching. Incredibly moving and breathtaking." —NY Daily News. "A sweet love letter of a play." —NY Times. "Wildly funny. Completely charming." —Star-Ledger. [1M, 1W] ISBN: 978-0-8222-2157-9

★ ICE GLEN by Joan Ackermann. In this touching period comedy, a beautiful poetess dwells in idyllic obscurity on a Berkshire estate with a band of unlikely cohorts. "A beautifully written story of nature and change." —Talkin' Broadway. "A lovely play which will leave you with a lot to think about." —CurtainUp. "Funny, moving and witty." —Metroland (Boston). [4M, 3W] ISBN: 978-0-8222-2175-3

★ THE LAST DAYS OF JUDAS ISCARIOT by Stephen Adly Guirgis. Set in a time-bending, darkly comic world between heaven and hell, this play reexamines the plight and fate of the New Testament's most infamous sinner. "An unforced eloquence that finds the poetry in lowdown street talk." —NY Times. "A real jaw-dropper." —Variety. "An extraordinary play." —Guardian (UK). [10M, 5W] ISBN: 978-0-8222-2082-4

DRAMATISTS PLAY SERVICE, INC.
440 Park Avenue South, New York, NY 10016 212-683-8960 Fax 212-213-1539
postmaster@dramatists.com   www.dramatists.com

NEW PLAYS

★ THE GREAT AMERICAN TRAILER PARK MUSICAL music and lyrics by David Nehls, book by Betsy Kelso. Pippi, a stripper on the run, has just moved into Armadillo Acres, wreaking havoc among the tenants of Florida's most exclusive trailer park. "Adultery, strippers, murderous ex-boyfriends, Costco and the Ice Capades. Undeniable fun." –*NY Post.* "Joyful and unashamedly vulgar." –*The New Yorker.* "Sparkles with treasure." –*New York Sun.* [2M, 5W] ISBN: 978-0-8222-2137-1

★ MATCH by Stephen Belber. When a young Seattle couple meet a prominent New York choreographer, they are led on a fraught journey that will change their lives forever. "Uproariously funny, deeply moving, enthralling theatre." –*NY Daily News.* "Prolific laughs and ear-to-ear smiles." –*NY Magazine.* [2M, 1W] ISBN: 978-0-8222-2020-6

★ MR. MARMALADE by Noah Haidle. Four-year-old Lucy's imaginary friend, Mr. Marmalade, doesn't have much time for her—not to mention he has a cocaine addiction and a penchant for pornography. "Alternately hilarious and heartbreaking." –*The New Yorker.* "A mature and accomplished play." –*LA Times.* "Scathingly observant comedy." –*Miami Herald.* [4M, 2W] ISBN: 978-0-8222-2142-5

★ MOONLIGHT AND MAGNOLIAS by Ron Hutchinson. Three men cloister themselves as they work tirelessly to reshape a screenplay that's just not working—*Gone with the Wind.* "Consumers of vintage Hollywood insider stories will eat up Hutchinson's diverting conjecture." –*Variety.* "A lot of fun." –*NY Post.* "A Hollywood dream-factory farce." –*Chicago Sun-Times.* [3M, 1W] ISBN: 978-0-8222-2084-8

★ THE LEARNED LADIES OF PARK AVENUE by David Grimm, translated and freely adapted from Molière's *Les Femmes Savantes.* Dicky wants to marry Betty, but her mother's plan is for Betty to wed a most pompous man. "A brave, brainy and barmy revision." –*Hartford Courant.* "A rare but welcome bird in contemporary theatre." –*New Haven Register.* "Roll over Cole Porter." –*Boston Globe.* [5M, 5W] ISBN: 978-0-8222-2135-7

★ REGRETS ONLY by Paul Rudnick. A sparkling comedy of Manhattan manners that explores the latest topics in marriage, friendships and squandered riches. "One of the funniest quip-meisters on the planet." –*NY Times.* "Precious moments of hilarity. Devastatingly accurate political and social satire." –*BackStage.* "Great fun." –*CurtainUp.* [3M, 3W] ISBN: 978-0-8222-2223-1

DRAMATISTS PLAY SERVICE, INC.
440 Park Avenue South, New York, NY 10016   212-683-8960   Fax 212-213-1539
postmaster@dramatists.com   www.dramatists.com

NEW PLAYS

★ **AFTER ASHLEY by Gina Gionfriddo.** A teenager is unwillingly thrust into the national spotlight when a family tragedy becomes talk-show fodder. "A work that virtually any audience would find accessible." *–NY Times.* "Deft characterization and caustic humor." *–NY Sun.* "A smart satirical drama." *–Variety.* [4M, 2W] ISBN: 978-0-8222-2099-2

★ **THE RUBY SUNRISE by Rinne Groff.** Twenty-five years after Ruby struggles to realize her dream of inventing the first television, her daughter faces similar battles of faith as she works to get Ruby's story told on network TV. "Measured and intelligent, optimistic yet clear-eyed." *–NY Magazine.* "Maintains an exciting sense of ingenuity." *–Village Voice.* "Sinuous theatrical flair." *–Broadway.com.* [3M, 4W] ISBN: 978-0-8222-2140-1

★ **MY NAME IS RACHEL CORRIE taken from the writings of Rachel Corrie, edited by Alan Rickman and Katharine Viner.** This solo piece tells the story of Rachel Corrie who was killed in Gaza by an Israeli bulldozer set to demolish a Palestinian home. "Heartbreaking urgency. An invigoratingly detailed portrait of a passionate idealist." *–NY Times.* "Deeply authentically human." *–USA Today.* "A stunning dramatization." *–CurtainUp.* [1W] ISBN: 978-0-8222-2222-4

★ **ALMOST, MAINE by John Cariani.** This charming midwinter night's dream of a play turns romantic clichés on their ear as it chronicles the painfully hilarious amorous adventures (and misadventures) of residents of a remote northern town that doesn't quite exist. "A whimsical approach to the joys and perils of romance." *–NY Times.* "Sweet, poignant and witty." *–NY Daily News.* "Aims for the heart by way of the funny bone." *–Star-Ledger.* [2M, 2W] ISBN: 978-0-8222-2156-2

★ **Mitch Albom's TUESDAYS WITH MORRIE by Jeffrey Hatcher and Mitch Albom, based on the book by Mitch Albom.** The true story of Brandeis University professor Morrie Schwartz and his relationship with his student Mitch Albom. "A touching, life-affirming, deeply emotional drama." *–NY Daily News.* "You'll laugh. You'll cry." *–Variety.* "Moving and powerful." *–NY Post.* [2M] ISBN: 978-0-8222-2188-3

★ **DOG SEES GOD: CONFESSIONS OF A TEENAGE BLOCKHEAD by Bert V. Royal.** An abused pianist and a pyromaniac ex-girlfriend contribute to the teen-angst of America's most hapless kid. "A welcome antidote to the notion that the *Peanuts* gang provides merely American cuteness." *–NY Times.* "Hysterically funny." *–NY Post.* "The *Peanuts* kids have finally come out of their shells." *–Time Out.* [4M, 4W] ISBN: 978-0-8222-2152-4

DRAMATISTS PLAY SERVICE, INC.
440 Park Avenue South, New York, NY 10016 212-683-8960 Fax 212-213-1539
postmaster@dramatists.com www.dramatists.com

NEW PLAYS

★ **RABBIT HOLE by David Lindsay-Abaire.** Winner of the 2007 Pulitzer Prize. Becca and Howie Corbett have everything a couple could want until a life-shattering accident turns their world upside down. "An intensely emotional examination of grief, laced with wit." *–Variety.* "A transcendent and deeply affecting new play." *–Entertainment Weekly.* "Painstakingly beautiful." *–BackStage.* [2M, 3W] ISBN: 978-0-8222-2154-8

★ **DOUBT, A Parable by John Patrick Shanley.** Winner of the 2005 Pulitzer Prize and Tony Award. Sister Aloysius, a Bronx school principal, takes matters into her own hands when she suspects the young Father Flynn of improper relations with one of the male students. "All the elements come invigoratingly together like clockwork." *–Variety.* "Passionate, exquisite, important, engrossing." *–NY Newsday.* [1M, 3W] ISBN: 978-0-8222-2219-4

★ **THE PILLOWMAN by Martin McDonagh.** In an unnamed totalitarian state, an author of horrific children's stories discovers that someone has been making his stories come true. "A blindingly bright black comedy." *–NY Times.* "McDonagh's least forgiving, bravest play." *–Variety.* "Thoroughly startling and genuinely intimidating." *–Chicago Tribune.* [4M, 5 bit parts (2M, 1W, 1 boy, 1 girl)] ISBN: 978-0-8222-2100-5

★ **GREY GARDENS book by Doug Wright, music by Scott Frankel, lyrics by Michael Korie.** The hilarious and heartbreaking story of Big Edie and Little Edie Bouvier Beale, the eccentric aunt and cousin of Jacqueline Kennedy Onassis, once bright names on the social register who became East Hampton's most notorious recluses. "An experience no passionate theatergoer should miss." *–NY Times.* "A unique and unmissable musical." *–Rolling Stone.* [4M, 3W, 2 girls] ISBN: 978-0-8222-2181-4

★ **THE LITTLE DOG LAUGHED by Douglas Carter Beane.** Mitchell Green could make it big as the hot new leading man in Hollywood if Diane, his agent, could just keep him in the closet. "Devastatingly funny." *–NY Times.* "An out-and-out delight." *–NY Daily News.* "Full of wit and wisdom." *–NY Post.* [2M, 2W] ISBN: 978-0-8222-2226-2

★ **SHINING CITY by Conor McPherson.** A guilt-ridden man reaches out to a therapist after seeing the ghost of his recently deceased wife. "Haunting, inspired and glorious." *–NY Times.* "Simply breathtaking and astonishing." *–Time Out.* "A thoughtful, artful, absorbing new drama." *–Star-Ledger.* [3M, 1W] ISBN: 978-0-8222-2187-6

DRAMATISTS PLAY SERVICE, INC.
440 Park Avenue South, New York, NY 10016 212-683-8960 Fax 212-213-1539
postmaster@dramatists.com www.dramatists.com